CW00543041

SHAKESPEARE COUNTRY

SHAKESPEARE COUNTRY

by Peter Whelan

WARNER CHAPPELL PLAYS

LONDON

A Time Warner Company

Shakespeare Country
First published in 1993
by Warner Chappell Plays Ltd
129 Park Street, London W1Y 3FA
Copyright © 1993 by Peter Whelan

ISBN 0 85676 165 6

Printed by Commercial Colour Press, London E7

FOREWORD

It was the first time I ever had an idea in church. About three years ago I was in Holy Trinity, Stratford, gazing at Shakespeare's tomb and musing on the thought that the Bard's family line died out completely in the eighteenth century. This saddened me . . . so I invented an illegitimate son who emigrated to America, to the new colony of Virginia. And this led me to Billy Shake.

As I thought about him he seemed to take on some of the qualities of Bottom in Midsummer Night's Dream. This was the time of the Velvet Revolution and the Berlin Wall coming down. I felt that a comedy of reconciliations, based on the Dream, was in order . . . though more recent conflicts have since cast their shadow, as you'll see in the play.

The trouble was it was a comedy . . . and I wasn't known for comedy. Writers can get type cast as well as actors. Also, I wondered whether the RSC was the right place to poke fun at what Sir Peter Hall has called the "Shakespeare Theme Park". So I was only too pleased when the Little Theatre Guild (that I've always been part of) gave me the chance to go out on a limb.

Of course, I couldn't follow the plot of the Dream in one essential: a story of lovers' relationships going awry can't easily end in wedding bells today . . . not when the very institution of marriage has gone awry. And that's when it began to get really interesting.

Peter Whelan
October, 1993

SHAKESPEARE COUNTRY was commissioned by British Telecom for the 1993 BT Biennial in association with the Little Theatre Guild of Great Britain, and was simultaneously premiered on 16th October, 1993 by the following theatres:

Robin Hood Theatre, Aversham
Bolton Little Theatre
New Venture Theatre, Brighton
Bromley Little Theatre
Carlisle Green Room Club
Miller Centre Players, Caterham
Chorley Amateur Dramatic & Operatic Society
Criterion Theatre, Coventry
Wharf Theatre, Devizes
Guild of Players, Dumfries
Questors Theatre, Ealing
Nomads, East Horsley
Caxton Players, Great Grimsby
Archway Theatre, Horley
Ilkley Players
Priory Theatre, Kenilworth
Loft Theatre, Leamington Spa
Lewes Theatre Club
Theatr Fach, Llangefni
Barn Theatre, Moulton
Apollo Theatre, Isle of Wight
Lacemarket Theatre, Nottingham
Oldbury Repertory Players
Progress Theatre, Reading
Richmond Shakespeare Society
Plaza Theatre, Romsey
Rugby Theatre
Studio Theatre, Salisbury
South London Theatre Centre
Stockport Garrick Theatre
Highbury Theatre, Sutton Coldfield
Sharon Players, Tel Aviv, Israel
Oast Theatre, Tonbridge
Lindley Players, Whitstable

Wokingham Theatre
Woodley Players, Reading
Workington Playgoers Club
Grove Park Little Theatre, Wrexham
Bangor Drama Club, N Ireland
Castle Players, Barnard Castle
Cardiff Little Theatre
Theatr Mwldan, Cardigan
Mayfield Players
GTC at Barton Green, New Malden
Cotswold Players, Stroud
Dylan Thomas Theatre, Swansea
Wilstead Players
Blackpool Theatre Company

CAST OF CHARACTERS

RAFE DUKE	Actor; 30-40
ZANA FERRIS	Actress; 30-40
BILLY SHAKE	American Country singer; 30-40
KOICHI BANDO	Japanese Executive/Spirit; 25-35
MIRA EDGE	Waitress, would-be actress; 20's
AURELIA WARD	Academic, Dame; 60's
GUNTER KAUFMANN	Academic, German; 60's
DAN HOWARD	Embattled Playwright; 20's
BONNY LEE	American, Billy's Manager; 30-40
WEBBO	A New Age Traveller & Spirit; Ageless
SERGEANT 405	A Soldier; 25-35

The time is the present.

The place is modern-day Stratford-upon-Avon, with its Shake-speare 'theme park' atmosphere.

ACT ONE

Scene One

Waterside, the street running by the river at Stratford-upon-Avon, the afternoon of a summer's day about now. RAFE, *an actor, is feeding the swans near the ferry landing stage.* ZANA, *an actress, is alongside him, nursing troubled thoughts.*

RAFE   I love this time of day in Stratford. From around five thirty-five, say, to half six or quarter to seven. The whole town drifts. The river slows down. You get that rattle of chains as shops stow away the awnings. A burst of bazouki as the taverna revs up for the night. And a miracle . . . d'you notice? For a brief half hour parking spaces appear in Bridge Street!

ZANA   I wish I were a tourist . . . just drinking in the day, up and down the town, in and out of the shops . . .

RAFE   Coming to the show . . .

ZANA   I mean no pressure. No being on the spot.

RAFE   Isn't an actor a kind of tourist? They pass through places. We pass through plays. If it's Tuesday it must be Coriolanus.

ZANA   I don't like that swan. It's looking at me.

RAFE   It's noticed your special aura. (*To the swan.*) You see her? You see this woman? This paragon? This goddess on earth? She has promised me that tomorrow morning she will become my lawful wedded wife. Wonderful traditional sound that has . . . lawful wedded wife.

ZANA   (*wryly*) Yes . . .

RAFE   (*to the swans*) Eleven o'clock, Holy Trinity church, just down river . . . bring your friends. (*To* ZANA.) They'll be there.

ZANA   Why not? Everyone else is coming . . .

RAFE   People just want to wish us well. You can't say 'no'.

ZANA   Every time I turn round there's another fifty guests!

RAFE   Nice to have full pews,

ZANA   We'll have ticket touts smuggling 'em in through the crypt. I don't mind relatives and friends but we'll have enemies in there!

RAFE   Nonsense! It's mostly the company.

ZANA   That's what I mean. That swan's got his eye on me again. He's saying, "Are you sure you're doing the right thing?"

RAFE   No he isn't!

ZANA   He's saying, "Nobody gets married these days".

RAFE   He is not!

ZANA   He's saying, "You've got along okay for two whole years sharing . . . why marry?"

RAFE   Look . . .

ZANA   He says, "Why let marriage destabilise a perfectly good live-in relationship?"

RAFE   If you're going to say something say it through me not through a swan!

ZANA   I thought if someone's going to stick their
        neck out it had better be him.

RAFE   (*to the swan*) What's she saying?

ZANA   Help. She's saying help.

RAFE   Brilliant!

ZANA   I do love you . . .

RAFE   Oh brilliant! Look, it's all happening and it's
        happening tomorrow. Half the town's coming
        . . . the press . . . even a couple of critics.

ZANA   Critics? Critics at your wedding!

RAFE   It was bound to go to everybody's heads . . .
        It's Oberon and Titania . . . it's the King and
        Queen of the fairies getting married.

ZANA   I thought they were married. Alright . . . I just
        need a space to think in. Tonight, after the
        show I won't come back to the flat. Don't
        argue. Tonight, you go your way . . . I'll go
        mine.

        (BILLY SHAKE *enters, stetson on head,
        belongings slung over his shoulder. He stares
        up into a tree for awhile.*)

BILLY   Howdy ma'am . . . sir. Tell me now. Is that a
        robin on yonder bough?

        (ZANA *and* RAFE *look up at the tree.*)

RAFE   Where?

BILLY   Right up top . . . no, she's gone. Ain't that the
        way? Birds don't stay still fer no one. Reason
        I ask is that I hear your British robin and our
        robin in the states are two total different
        species. The only likeness is they both have
        red breasts.

RAFE   Is that the case?

BILLY   So I do hear . . .

ZANA   Well . . . Is this your first time in Stratford?

BILLY   First time in England. Got out at Heathrow
                an' hitched me a ride. Didn't waste a minute . . .
                no sir! Had to see Stratford upon the Avon
                jes' as soon as I could.

RAFE   Where are you from?

BILLY   Virginia. Born in Texas, raised in Virginia.
                When my granpappy who raised me mostly . . .
                when he died this year, I said ter myself,
                Billy, you got to go see William
                Shakespeare's own country . . . Jes' like your
                granpappy would have like you to do. Oh he
                revered Shakespeare, sir . . . ma'am . . . he
                really did.

ZANA   Are you going to the play tonight?

BILLY   Now which of the cannon would that one be?

RAFE   A Midsummer Night's Dream.

BILLY   I'll be darned! That's my all-time favourite.
                If I got hit over the head an' woke up in the
                mornin' an' someone said, "Billy you jes'
                wrote one of Will Shakespeare's plays", I'd
                say, "I jes' hope it's Midsummer Night's
                Dream" 'cos that'd be the one I'd most want
                it to be . . . "But we are spirits of another
                sort. I with the morning's love have oft made
                sport. And like a forester the groves may
                tread, even to the Eastern gate all fiery-red."

RAFE   (*very pleased at him doing Oberon*) Very
                good! Listen my friend. I hear it's sold out . . .
                but I'll be glad to provide a ticket. Is it just
                one you want? It's a complimentary. Nothing
                to pay.

BILLY	Well that's real kind. That's generous, sir!
RAFE	Just one thing in return. Look at this lady . . . and at me . . .
ZANA	Rafe . . .
RAFE	And tell me - do we belong together?
ZANA	Oh my!
BILLY	Well . . . I'll answer you, sir. Lookin' at you both I'd say you had a shine about you "Like unto the shine of twin drops of dew that must fall upon the selfsame leaf and so run together."
RAFE	Thank you, friend . . . Billy.
ZANA	(*aside*) Was that Shakespeare?
	(KOICHI *enters. Stylish summer clothes, maps, video camcorder, etc. He holds the Midsummer Night's Dream programme.*)
KOICHI	Miss Zana Ferris and Mr Rafe Duke. I recognise you from your pics. I'd be always in your debt for your autographs.
ZANA	You saw the show?
KOICHI	I saw you! When you first are revealed on the stage there is a shimmer in the air, over the audience . . . like threads of fire. I think then that all kinds of magic are possible.
RAFE	You mean her . . .
KOICHI	No sir. You. (*To* ZANA.) And you. It was real neat.
ZANA	Thank you. Shall I put your name?

KOICHI	Koichi . . . Koichi Bando. But you just write Koichi. K-O-I-C-H-I. Great!
ZANA	"To Koichi who appreciates magic".

(*She writes and signs, as does* RAFE.)

BILLY	(*to* KOICHI) Shake, Mr Koichi.

(*They shake hands.*)

Do I understand from this that the lady and gentleman act in the play?

KOICHI	You are with Oberon and Titania.
BILLY	The King and Queen of the Fairies?
KOICHI	The same.
BILLY	An' you the first folk I met in Stratford!
RAFE	Tonight's a special night for the play . . . it's midsummer eve.
KOICHI	Yes, I know. I have promised myself that tonight I will commune with the spirit of Shakespeare . . . at the famous oak tree in the woods.
ZANA	Shakespeare's oak? Be careful. It might not exist.
KOICHI	Oh yes. He sat under it to write his first attempts at poetry. I know where it is . . .
BILLY	In that case, sir, I'd be greatly obliged if you'd tell me how I could find it.
KOICHI	(*points*) Three miles that direction, in the wood.

(*They all look in the direction* KOICHI *points to. As they do, he does a quick slight bow and exits, so that when they look back he has disappeared.*)

ZANA Where? Oh . . . he's gone!

RAFE What did he do? Jump in the river?

BILLY Plum disappeared! I'll be durned!

RAFE Look . . . we'll have to go . . .

ZANA Oh yes!

RAFE I'll put your ticket at the stage door. (*Points.*) Anyone'll direct you . . .

(MIRA *has entered, on her way to work.*)

MIRA I'll show him, Rafe!

(RAFE *is halted as he is going. He doesn't recognise her. Neither does* ZANA.)

RAFE (*vaguely*) Thanks.

MIRA You don't remember me, do you? You came to our drama school, Studio Stage . . . You did a master class . . .

RAFE (*not recalling*) Ah, yes!

MIRA I was Juliet to your Romeo . . .

ZANA (*aside*) Here we go!

RAFE Of course! Brilliant!

MIRA (*doggedly*) Perhaps you could put in a word. I've almost got an interview.

RAFE Brilliant! Hang in there . . . give it your best shot!

ZANA (*aside*) Jesus!

RAFE Billy . . . I'll leave your ticket in the name of Billy . . . ?

BILLY   Shake . . .

             (RAFE *rushes back to shake his hand.*)

             That's my name . . . "Shake".

RAFE   Shake, Brilliant!

             (*He rushes away with* ZANA.)

MIRA   (*calls after him*) The name's Mira Edge . . .
             Brightest talent of her generation you poncy
             git! (*Disgusted.*) Give it your best shot . . .

BILLY   Howdy . . .

MIRA   Hi.

BILLY   Tell me . . . Is that a robin on yonder bough?

MIRA   A what? Where?

BILLY   A robin, on the topmost twig.

MIRA   Dunno. I don't know birds. They're the things
             with feathers on aren't they?

BILLY   Jes' me wantin' to see a British robin to
             remind me of the American robin. Feelin'
             homesick, I guess.

MIRA   How long you been over here then?

BILLY   Arrived this mornin' . . .

             (*He has broken the ice. She grins.*)

MIRA   I don't have a home. I have rooms. Home is
             where my next nervous breakdown is.

BILLY   Tell you one thing about you. You gotta be an
             actress.

MIRA   Oh?

BILLY	You got that shine about you . . .
MIRA	Wouldn't be because I just said I was, would it?
BILLY	(*grins*) That too.
MIRA	No I'm knocking on the door to get in. Working behind the counter till I can get an interview.
BILLY	Maybe I'll join you.
MIRA	What?
BILLY	Need the dough.
MIRA	Americans always have dough.
BILLY	Not this one. Lost all my money on the plane to Heathrow.
MIRA	Didn't they look for it? You can't lose your money on a plane.
BILLY	Can if there's a poker school.
MIRA	Listen, if you're stuck for a meal tonight I work at a burger joint just down the road. Come around eleven. Manager leaves me to finish off and lock up. I can slip you a free burger.
BILLY	Now ain't people kind in this country? Free ride, free show, free meal!
MIRA	See the scenery van over there? That's the door for your ticket. I'm down that way at Willie's Burger Bar. In honour of Willie . . . you know. We sell Willieburgers. They're like normal burgers only instead of being round they're shaped like a Willie.
BILLY	Yee haw! Do like a female with a sense o' humour! Just you make sure you get that actress job, you hear?

MIRA   Not actress. That's sexist. Actors are actors.
                Some have something between their legs . . .
                and some have something between their ears!

                (*She exits.*)

BILLY   Yee haw! Well . . . here I am granpappy . . .
                an' it sure is a dandy prospect. Ol' stone
                walls, green green grass, flowers hangin' in
                the air . . . and them white swans of Avon.
                Shakespeare Country!

                (*As he speaks, you have the option: take lights
                down for the end of the scene, or bring in
                music for the song, either solo guitar or a
                small country music combo. This can be
                onstage, such as a group of passing tourists,
                or offstage. The band or additional singers
                can help with the chorus.*)

(*Sings*)   Li'l old town by a river
                Weepin' willer trees
                Cats all sittin' in the grass
                Eatin' strawberries
                Shakespeare's flag a flyin'
                Up in the clear blue sky
                Come to Shakespeare Country
                Gotter see it afore you die

(*Chorus*)   Shakespeare Country!
                Of thee I dream
                Shakespeare Country!
                It's poetry . . . an' cream

                            2
                Honey coloured houses
                Houses black and white
                Sun shines on the ol' red rooves
                Such a purdy sight
                But a man here asked the question
                To be or not to be
                An' he made Shakespeare Country
                The place to be fer me . . .

(*Chorus*)

3
Them Shakespeare dudes is goin'
Ter see a Shakespeare play
Walkin' by the water
On a summer's day
If only William Shakespeare
Would come strollin' by
Back to Shakespeare Country
So I could jes' say "Hi" . . .

(*Chorus as lights fade for the end of the
scene.*)

Scene Two

*A few minutes later on the front patio of The Black Swan pub
. . . more famously known as The Dirty Duck. One or two
benches, a Dirty Duck sign and leafy lighting. The entrance
to the pub can be off-stage. The only drinker is* DAME AURELIA
WARD. *She sips Campari and studies a copy of the
Shakespeare Quarterly. A barman could be flicking tables
and collecting glasses. Presently* GUNTER KAUFMANN *enters
from the street. He beams with delight as he sees* AURELIA . . .
who is not immediately aware of his presence.

GUNTER   Who is this, sitting, as she said she would,
              outside the famous Dirty Duck and looking
              like the girl I left behind me in 1955?

AURELIA   1954 . . . August.

GUNTER   Aurelia!

AURELIA   Gunter!

GUNTER   If you are the real Aurelia I claim you with
              this kiss.

              (*He kisses her . . . fondly.*)

AURELIA   Hmm. You seem to be the real Gunter . . .

GUNTER   No, no, I am not what I am. I am not the Herr
                Professor of European Literature . . . I am a
                young German boy of half a lifetime ago who
                came to Stratford to study Shakespeare and in
                this town met the young Englishwoman of his
                dreams. Now I meet her again.

AURELIA   Changed by time . . .

GUNTER   No. We will not allow time the smallest
                victory. I was excited like a child to get your
                letter, especially to learn, did I read it
                correctly . . . that you are free once more?

AURELIA   If you mean that I am part of that
                contemporary English social phenomenon the
                grandparental divorcee . . . yes I am.

GUNTER   Then I shall kiss you in the old way . . .

                (*He begins to do so, but she evades.*)

AURELIA   Gunter! I am a governor of the Royal
                Shakespeare Company . . . not to mention a
                Fellow of Wadham College!

GUNTER   Then I shall get the drinks.

                (*A* BARMAN *appears with a pint.* AURELIA *takes
                it and hands it to* GUNTER *as the* BARMAN *exits
                into the pub.*)

AURELIA   All taken care of. I told them to draw it when
                you arrived.

GUNTER   I could weep real tears! You remembered. My
                pint of English wallop!

AURELIA   Well that word dates you for a start.

GUNTER   To the fifties!

AURELIA   The fifties!

GUNTER   See you later alligator!

AURELIA   In a while crocodile! Now I've ordered dinner
          here so we can relax a moment and have a
          chat about the latest state of Shakepearian
          scholarship and what have you.

          (GUNTER *picks up the "Quarterly".*)

GUNTER   Ah . . . I see you are reading Doctor Celia
          Dymchurch on "Shakespeare and Foot
          Fetishism"?

AURELIA   Ludicrous!

GUNTER   And Sommerfield on "Some Anal Retentive
          Aspects of Hamlet".

AURELIA   Crap!

GUNTER   Oh just to think of us all those years ago
          walking by the river there . . . going to
          theatre . . .

AURELIA   We saw King Lear . . .

GUNTER   Don't mention King Lear . . . They say you
          notice your age when policemen look younger
          . . . for me it's when the King Lears look
          younger. So. How is the Royal Shakespeare
          Company?

AURELIA   Not well at all. I'm afraid we're facing a
          financial crisis.

GUNTER   Again?

AURELIA   Again.

GUNTER   What caused it this time?

AURELIA   Mainly getting over the last financial crisis . . .
          (*Pause.*) What happened to your wife?

GUNTER	She went off to live with a member of the European Parliament. The worst of it was I'd just voted for him. And your husband?
AURELIA	He's re-married . . . to Professor Alice Meynard, author of "Shakespeare's Hidden Intentions".
	(BILLY *enters from The Waterside during this. He nods to them amicably.*)
BILLY	Hi there!
BOTH	(*uncertainly*) Hello . . .
BILLY	I wonder would you assist me . . . ma'am . . . sir. Tell me, is that a robin on yonder bough? (*He points.*)
AURELIA	No. It's a nuthatch. Blue back. White breast. Yes, nuthatch! Interesting etymology. "Hatch" does not mean "hatch" as we mean "hatch", as in hatching an egg . . . no, no, no! The nuthatch, you see, breaks open nuts with its beak . . . so the "hatch" in "nuthatch" refers to a verb fallen into disuse, though I'm told still lingering on in some remote areas, which is the verb from the noun "hatchet" . . . "to hatch", therefore, meaning "to chop".
BILLY	Gee!
GUNTER	This is good information my friend. You are speaking to Dame Aurelia Ward, author of "Shakespeare's Birdlife".
AURELIA	Please don't embarrass me . . .
BILLY	Dame? You're a Dame?
AURELIA	Strictly in the British sense!
BILLY	An' would you be one of these-here Shakespeare Experts?

GUNTER   Oh she certainly is!

AURELIA   As is Dr Kaufman, author of "Shakespeare's
                German Connection" and "The German
                Origins of Shakespeare's Mother".

GUNTER   Who was not, as is ignorantly supposed, Mary
                Arden but Maria Hartmann from Oberhausen
                in Nordrhein Westfalen!

                (*During this* DAN HOWARD *has come out on the
                patio from the pub, with a pint and a copy of
                the* Stage. *He sits at another bench but his
                attention is drawn by what* BILLY *has to say.*)

BILLY   Ain't that my lucky break? I was lookin' fer
                Shakespeare experts on account of bein', if
                what my granpappy allus told me was correct,
                a direct descendant of William Shakespeare!

                (AURELIA *and* GUNTER *exchange wary glances.*)

AURELIA   Of Shakespeare?

BILLY   Yes ma'am.

GUNTER   What might lead you to suppose such a thing?

BILLY   Well it was passed down my family line fer
                four hundred years that a son of the great
                William Shakespeare crossed to the new
                world to find his fortune an' put down roots
                right where my granpappy lived in Virginia.

AURELIA   How splendid. You must excuse us now . . .
                we have a table booked for dinner . . .

                (*She nudges a gobsmacked* GUNTER *into life.
                They both stand.*)

                I think you'll find that Shakespeare's
                offspring all died in this country and that the
                entire family line ceased in the eighteenth
                century.

BILLY   Sure did, Ma'am. But that was the legitimate
             line. I'm talkin' of the illegitimate line, beg
             pardon ma'am . . . like my ancestor was the
             bastard son of the Bard.

AURELIA   (*frosty*) I see . . .

BILLY   Which is how I got my family name . . .
             "Shake".

GUNTER   Shake?

BILLY   Billy Shake. See, my ancestor, bein' a
             bastard, felt he was only entitled to half the
             name.

AURELIA   Time to go in.

             (*But* GUNTER *is beginning to get interested.*)

GUNTER   There were certainly rumours of illicit issue . . .

BILLY   An' here you see one of the rumours standing
             on its own two feet, sir! I always think of that
             line in King Lear.

GUNTER   (*nervous*) King Lear?

BILLY   When Edmund says, "Now Gods stand up fer
             bastards!" I feel that's Shakespeare rootin' fer
             me! Not that I'm a bastard myself. My parents
             may not have been married when I was born
             but they'd only been divorced twelve months.

AURELIA   Gunter . . .

GUNTER   Ja . . . coming . . . I like your story, Mr
             Shake. May I buy you a beer?

BILLY   That'd be most appreciated, sir. Sure would.

             (GUNTER *and* AURELIA *exit to the pub,* GUNTER
             still amused and fascinated. DAN *applauds*
             BILLY. *He is all admiration for what he sees
             as a smooth con trick.*)

DAN   (*to* BILLY) That was great! You just got
           yourself a beer!

BILLY   Real nice folks.

DAN   I mean that was numero uno! I really hand it
           to you. You make it all look so easy. They
           may not have believed you but they were
           hooked.

BILLY   Ain't nuthin' but the gospel truth, sir.

DAN   Dan Howard. I'm proud to meet such a master
           of the art.

BILLY   You visitin' Stratford, Dan?

DAN   Me visit Stratford? No . . . I hate the place.
           It's not a town it's a Shakespeare theme park.
           It's for people with half-timbered minds. Bric
           a brac land. Coach loads of wrinklies pouring
           into Edinburgh Woollen Mills to buy grandma
           a Black Watch kilt. My curse on its poncy
           flower beds and manicured lawns. May its
           river fill with turds and its hills resound to the
           sound of farting.

BILLY   Well, that's a kinda new slant on it Dan . . .

DAN   Wouldn't be here at all if I didn't have to be.
           I'm a playwright . . . I'm here trying to get
           them to take one of my plays.

BILLY   Gee! A genuine living playwright!

DAN   We're not all dead! Mind you, all they really
           want here is Big Willy. Being a playwright in
           Stratford's like being in Madonna's chorus
           line. You see what I want to give 'em is a
           hard, uncompromising look at the scabby
           underbelly of Britain today . . .

           (GUNTER *appears from the pub with a pint.*)

GUNTER   Bitte schön, my friend!

BILLY   Thank you sir, most kindly.

GUNTER   (*secretive*) Your ancestor, Mr Shake . . .
                would you, perhaps, know his first name?

BILLY   Surely do. It was Wilbur.

GUNTER   (*suppressing amusement*) Wilbur Shakespeare!

BILLY   No. Wilbur Shake.

GUNTER   Danke! Wunderschön! Wilbur Shake!

                (*He exits to the pub, gleefully.*)

DAN   Great! He thinks he's got you. But you got
                him! Cheers!

BILLY   Cheers, Dan. (*Drinks.*) Saved my life. I don't
                have a single dime to buy a club soda!

DAN   You too? Look . . . this is all I have spare in
                the world. A new 5p piece. The original groat.
                Visible symbol of Britain's decline.

BILLY   All I got in my pocket is a ticket fer
                Midsummer Night's Dream.

                (*He shows it.* DAN *is excited.*)

DAN   So you have!

BILLY   Real nice guy give it me . . . on the house.

DAN   But the Dream's sold out tonight! This is
                worth gold! Let's see . . . Band A! That's near
                on thirty quid! You can sell that in a flash. Its
                harder currency than the Saudi Arabian riyad!

BILLY   Kinda set my heart on seein' that play . . .

DAN   No! It's all done in a scrap metal yard with
                stainless steel fairies. You must be hungry.

You've money there for a meal and enough
left over for a bottle of . . . what's your
favourite drink?

BILLY   Wild Turkey! The real Tennessee!

DAN   (*vaguely*) Yeah . . . even that.

BILLY   But I bin offered a free burger by a sassy
             young gal I met by the river.

DAN   A Willieburger?

BILLY   Yup . . .

DAN   No . . . I wouldn't go for that. I have to tell
             you I know the girl in question and you
             wouldn't stand a chance. She happens to be
             my lady. Oh . . . she wouldn't want to turn
             you down but, between you and me, she's
             serially monogamous . . .

BILLY   (*shaken*) Jeez!

             (KOICHI *enters from the pub. He sees* DAN
             waving BILLY'S *ticket.*)

DAN   So . . . all we need is a buyer for the ticket.

KOICHI   Greetings!

             (*They are startled by his sudden appearance.*)

             If it is for tonight I am over the moon to take
             it off your hands. Band A . . . Here is fifty
             pounds.

BILLY   (*still amazed*) Ain't got no change Mr Koichi . . .

KOICHI   That does not matter. Poetry has no price, Mr
             Shake.

             (KOICHI *turns to go.*)

BILLY   Knows my name! Hey Mr Koichi!
             Shakespeare's oak . . . can you tell me the
             direction again?

KOICHI   (*gives a slip of paper*) This is the Great Bear.
             Look for it tonight. Where the line through
             these two stars meets earth is the wood. In the
             wood, the oak.

             (KOICHI *exits to waterside*.)

DAN   Fifty quid?

BILLY   Great Bear . . . Shakespeare's oak.

DAN   Forget Shakespeare's oak! There's probably
             two thousand of them all round Stratford and
             since he was such a friggin' genius he
             probably sat under them all! You're going to
             have dinner at the Duck my friend. May I
             suggest the house speciality "Cluck and
             Duck" . . . that's chicken and duck in equal
             parts washed down with Wild Turkey and
             finish on Midsummer Dream pie and cream.
             And since you may get lonely I'll accompany
             you on a packet of bread sticks and four
             Newcastle Browns.

BILLY   Real kind of you, Dan!

             (DAN *leads* BILLY *into song*.)

DAN   If you're lookin' for a place to eat
             I'm tellin' you that you're in luck . . .
             Everyone on the Stratford beat
             Has dinner at the Duck . . .

BOTH   People all around the world
             Know this hostelrie
             From Sydney, Stuttgart, Paris, Rome,
             Tokyo and New York City . . .

             Here's the place you'll see the stars
             Havin' dinner at the Duck.
             Come and mingle in the bars . . .
             Dinner at the Duck

Where every bite
Is an opening night
And your taste buds get stage struck!
Quack - quack . . . quack, quack, quack . . .
Dinner at the Duck.

*   *   *

Dinner . . . dinner . . .
Dinner at the Duck . . .
Dinner . . . you won't get thinner . . .
Dinner at the Duck!

Hamlet, Falstaff, Rosalind . . .
They've all eaten here
You may see Cordelia
Buyin' a beer for ol' King Lear!

Sit right down and take your ease
For dinner at the Duck . . .
They're callin' for "beginners please"
Dinner at the Duck . . .

DAN   Your hors d'eouvre
           Is ready to serve . . .

BILLY   Soup of the day
           On its way . . .

DAN   Melon an' ham
           And a sole Bonne Femme . . .
           Then should you prefer
           Chicken chasseur . . .

BILLY   Well . . . I'm gonna take
           A T-Bone steak
           Big enough to fill a truck

BOTH   Quack - quack . . . quack, quack, quack
           We're havin' dinner . . . dinner . . .
           Dinner at the Duck!

(They exit into the pub. The lights fade.)

Scene Three

Night. Around eleven o'clock outside Willie's Burger Bar.
The light shines from the doorway. MIRA, *in uniform, waits.*
Overhead a "W" sign shines, like a McDonald's "M", but
upside down. ZANA *enters, walking in deep thought after the*
show. She sits on a bench.

MIRA   Hello, Miss Ferris.

ZANA   (*startled*) Oh! I remember you . . .

MIRA   That's more than Rafe Duke did.

ZANA   I think it came back to him later . . .

MIRA   Great! Would you like a Willieburger?

ZANA   No thanks. I'm getting married in twelve
            hours time. (*Realises.*) Ah . . . I didn't mean
            to make that connection. I've just got
            wedding on the mind. When's your interview?

MIRA   I dunno. I made that up. This is what I do.

ZANA   I used to work in Spud-U-Like. Then a spell
            as a Tudor serving wench at Ye Groaning
            Board in Kensington. Ye Groping Board,
            more like. All the businessmen had codpieces
            velcroed onto their pinstripes. A time to hold
            onto your wassail bowl with both hands.

MIRA   Have a free tea.

ZANA   Yeh!

            (MIRA *goes into the burger bar. Presently we*
            hear her call out.)

MIRA   (*off*) Shouldn't you be at a party or
            something?

ZANA   Possibly. But I'm not. I need thinking time.

(MIRA *enters with two take-away cups of tea.*)

MIRA   Really?

ZANA   Have to psyche myself up. Thanks . . . is this
            alright?

MIRA   Yeh. Manager goes home to his loved ones
            and leaves me to lock up. It's going to be a
            big affair . . . everyone's talking about it . . .
            your wedding.

ZANA   Would you like a big wedding?

MIRA   Me? Doubt if I'll ever have a small one. It
            should be quick really, shouldn't it? Like
            getting passport photos in one of those photo
            booths. Marriage booths. Should have them at
            stations. You put a coin in and both sit down . . .
            draw the curtain . . . and a picture of a vicar
            comes up on the screen and says, "I now
            pronounce you man and wife." Kiss! Flash!
            Photo. All done.

ZANA   If the world is full of broken vows, what's the
            good of adding to them? Vow no more vows!
            Then, at least, we'd have none to break.

MIRA   My parents have split.

ZANA   So have mine. And they had a big wedding.
            Can't we just be friends and lovers and be left
            in peace? Why does it have to be done in such
            a pompous way? It's as though they want to
            take it out of your hands. Fate! Destiny!
            Marriages are made in heaven! Though why
            should they think that? Everyone up there's
            dead.

MIRA   I shan't marry. I've got a boyfriend . . . if you
            can call him a boyfriend. I don't call him a
            boyfriend. But then . . . what the hell is a
            boyfriend these days? Personally I've never
            had one that works.

ZANA   What doesn't he do?

MIRA   He's a playwright.

ZANA   Say no more!

MIRA   And they've rejected his play!

ZANA   Never marry a playwright!

MIRA   Especially a rejected playwright! They don't
            need a woman. They need a scratching post!

ZANA   What's his name?

MIRA   Dan Howard.

ZANA   Oh I've heard of him. Didn't he do one with
            Northern Tub Thump? What was it called?

MIRA   "Gunge". He always uses titles like that. The
            latest is called "Sewage".

ZANA   What's it about?

MIRA   (*quotes*) "The scandalous neglect of our
            sewage infrastructure". He sets it in 2010 AD.
            All the pipes have burst and Britain is
            swimming in excreta . . .

ZANA   Symbolic . . .

MIRA   There's a part for me . . . a tough, socially
            conscious health worker on a very high horse.
            "Councillor Grimble! Look what your lot
            have brought us to. An entire city up to its
            neck in shit! Sewer rats in the old people's
            sheltered accommodation and the library lost
            in a lake of piss." He wants me to do it for my
            audition.

ZANA   Be a change from Juliet's balcony scene.

MIRA	That's what he thinks I am . . . tough. Uncompromising. But I just want someone to say, "Darling, you're wonderful". Preferably a director . . . but I wouldn't mind it from Dan.

(BONNY *enters on a short fuse.*)

BONNY	Howdy!
MIRA	Sorry, we're closed.
BONNY	Have you ladies seen a man around here?
ZANA	What sort?
BONNY	Like a walkin' Virginia ham with an apple and cinnamon smile an' he's a big, dumb bum an' he's late!
MIRA	Billy?
BONNY	That's him! Should ha' showed up six hour ago at the Shakespeare Hotel . . . skid-row trash!
ZANA	You're his wife?
BONNY	Wife? Haw! Haw! Haw! Marry him? Jes' as soon marry a male rattlesnake . . . if there is male an' female in rattlesnakes. Guess there must be . . . though I don't rightly see how. Anyways. I'm not Billy's wife, I'm his manager. Bonny Lee of Lee an' Lee Associates. The Lee an' Lee bein' me an' me.

(*Hands out cards.*)

I tell yer the only partnership you can trust in this world is a partnership with yourself. May not be legal but by God it works!

ZANA	This says "music management".

BONNY   Country style. Billy passes fer a singer when he's not too drunk or stoned. I tell yer honey . . .

ZANA   I'm Zana . . . this is Mira . . .

BONNY   I tell yer, Zana an' Mira, all I'm married to with any man is my percentage.

                  (BONNY *leads them into song.*)

(*Sings*)   Where the bee sucks there suck I
                  In a cowslip's bell I lie
                  An' I'm not givin' that up fer any guy . . .
                  Nonny nonny no!

                  It was a lover an' his lass
                  That o'er the green cornfields did pass
                  She said "Marriage? Stick it up yer ass!"
                  Nonny nonny no . . .

(*Chorus*)   Hey nonny nonny
                  The single life is bonny
                  So if he asks yer honey
                  Say nonny nonny no!
                  Nonny no . . . nonny no . . .
                  If he asks yer honey say
                  Nonny nonny no.

                          2
                  Now if Tom bears logs into your hall
                  And Dick the shepherd blows his nail an' all
                  Jes' tell 'em you-all ain't availaball . . .
                  Nonny nonny no.

                  Is tu-whit tu-woo a merry note
                  While greasy Joan doth keel the pote?
                  Godammit the sonuvabitches can keel their
                                         own pote
                  Nonny nonny no!

                          3
ZANA   But if he says what is mine is yours
                  And I'll wash the dishes and do the chores . . .

BONNY	Honey . . . there ain't no Santa Claus
ALL	Nonny nonny no!
MIRA	But marriage is more than sharin' a duvet It's bein' one flesh . . . that could be groovay
BONNY	Sounds like more to me like a horror moovay!
ALL	Nonny nonny no

(*After second chorus, a slower verse with a sadder note.*)

Hey ho the wind and the rain
Wimmin is wimmin and men is main
Maybe one day they'll git together agin' . . .

(*Pause.*)

But not till we has our fill o' livin
Nonny nonny no!

(*A final chorus.*)

BONNY	Jeez . . . here he is now.

(BILLY *and* DAN *enter, full of good cheer.*)

Billy Shake . . . you stood me up you bastard!

BILLY	Hiya, Bonny! I jus' ate the purdiest meal you ever did see. There was real, genuine old oak beams . . .
BONNY	Well I did hear things was bad in this clapped out country but I didn't think they wuz down ter eatin' wood!

(*She turns her back on him.*)

DAN	(*guilty*) Hi Mira. He won't need his Willieburger.

MIRA   (*angry*) Nor will you!

                (MIRA, *likewise, turns her back on* DAN.)

BILLY   (*seeing* ZANA) Hi Mizz Zana!

ZANA   Hi . . . enjoy the show?

BILLY   Ah . . . well . . . got kinda sidetracked . . .

BONNY   There are some people's lives are an apology
                jes' fer bein' here . . . but Billy's life is an
                unendin' apology fer not bein' nowhere . . .
                nowhere at all!

ZANA   Yes . . . well I think I shall wander . . .

DAN   Zana Ferris? The pre-wedding party's in full
                cry at the Duck. They'd just carried out one
                of the bell ringers . . .

ZANA   I'd better give it a miss. Don't want to be sick
                on the altar steps. I shall contemplate the
                night sky and commune with the stars . . .

BILLY   Why don't you go an' commune with
                Shakespeare's oak this Midsummer Night,
                Mizz Zana? You find that by the stars . . .

                (*He finds the Great Bear and does a line
                down from it.*)

                Right in the middle of that wood.

ZANA   I remember that wood. It's where Rafe and I
                used to walk in the old times . . . when all we
                were was two people in love. Yes . . . thank
                you. That's where I'll go. Sleep well
                everyone.

                (*She exits.* MIRA *has an urge to go with her.*)

DAN   (*to* MIRA) Okay Mira . . . where's the french
                fries?

MIRA (*angry with him*) Zana! Zana! I'll come with you!

(*She rushes to lock up.*)

DAN What did I say?

MIRA You think you can saunter in, any old time, snap your fingers an' here I am to put food in your mouth and dole out the dosh. I'm going to have an intelligent conversation for a change! Zana! Wait for me, Zana!

(*She exits.*)

DAN (*to* BILLY) Well, we'll have to contemplate the oak tree on our own Billy.

BONNY (*to* BILLY) Who is this guy? You ain't been givin' away secrets or doin' deals behind Bonny's back, have you Billy?

BILLY You know me, honey. Only deals I do is with a deck of cards . . .

(RAFE *enters, breathless and limping.*)

RAFE Where's Zana? Was she here? I heard her name . . .

BILLY Jes' takin' a stroll under the stars, Rafe . . .

RAFE She's what?

DAN It's okay. Mira's with her . . .

RAFE Where's she gone?

BONNY (*loud, impatient with all of this*) She's walkin' in the woods!

RAFE What?

BILLY Them woods over there . . . jes' outer town.

RAFE

But I must speak to her, I must get her back! Hell, I can't walk! My legs have gone!

(RAFE *hobbles about.*)

BILLY

You got trouble, Rafe?

RAFE

I got half crippled on stage tonight. Peaseblossom caught her wand between my legs and I went arse over tit into this stainless steel dock leaf on springs that our bloody designer saddled us with . . . but you were there . . . you saw me . . .

(*Before* BILLY *can explain* KOICHI *enters and is at* RAFE'S *side, unnoticed.*)

KOICHI

I would be happy to provide transport Mr Duke . . .

RAFE

Koichi! You can give me a lift?

KOICHI

Sure can, Mr Duke. My wheels are just in the next street . . .

RAFE

Brilliant! (*Heartfelt.*) You may save my marriage.

KOICHI

Lean on me, Mr Duke.

(*They exit.*)

DAN

Hello, hello! He seems to have had it up to here with playing Oberon. I'll give him my play to read. There's a good part for him as a hard hitting sanitary engineer who knows how to fight dirty and does. That's what he should be doing . . . finger on the pulse stuff . . . straight for the jugular. And they turn it down! I ask you. What Stratford wants is more of the kind of plays that Stratford doesn't want!

BONNY

You really is fulla shit, ain't yer. Billy! I wanna talk business . . .

(But they are interrupted by AURELIA *and* GUNTER *who now enter, amused to see* BILLY.)

GUNTER   Ah, Mr Shake! Enjoying the scenes of your ancestor's childhood?

BILLY   Sure am, Doctor Kaufmann . . . I sure am.

AURELIA   This name "Wilbur" . . . could it possibly have been "Wilobie", a name thought to refer to Shakespeare in a satire on him that depicted him in a farcical extra-marital sexual escapade?

GUNTER   *(pursuing the joke)* Or could it have been "Willmore"? Then it would link with Shakespeare's sonnet 135 *(He quotes.)* "So thou, being rich in Will, add to thy Will one Will of mine to make thy large Will more" . . . You see, "Willmore".

AURELIA   *(laughs)* Fabulous! It's a pun, you understand, on Shakespeare's name "Will" and the word "Will", which in Elizabethan English meant the male and female genitalia!

            (She and GUNTER *laugh uproariously.* BONNY *is not amused.)*

BONNY   Do I take it, Billy, that you have appraised this lady and gentleman of certain facts concerning your antecedents?

BILLY   Sure did Bonny. This lady is Dame Aurelia Ward and this is Doctor Kaufman . . . and they are genuine, bona-fide Shakespearean experts . . . jes like we wuz lookin' fer!

BONNY   *(interested)* Is that so?

BILLY   You heard 'em jus' now . . .

            *(*BONNY *changes her attitude.)*

BONNY

Well now. Pull up a park bench an' lets talk this thing over in a civilised modus vivendi.

GUNTER

(*alarmed, sensing his destiny with* AURELIA *in peril*) We must get on our way back to the hotel . . .

AURELIA

(*a touch embarrassed*) Oh we can surely spare a moment if there's something we can help with.

BONNY

That's real kind . . . an' I'm sure your kindness will not go unrewarded 'cos when the world gets ter hear what we come to this town to reveal it's going to blow the lid right off Stratford by the Avon. That man . . . (*She nods at* BILLY.) . . . may not look much but I tell you he's a walking stick of dynamite.

GUNTER

(*still wanting to get* AURELIA *to himself*) But we know his story already.

BONNY

Did you tell 'em about the box?

BILLY

Nope.

AURELIA

Box?

DAN

Box?

BONNY

(*dropping the mask of sweetness*) Listen Dan. If you didn't already know somethin' I wouldn't deal you in but understand that this matter is sub-judice and sine diem. So keep that sneerin' Limey lip buttoned tight, 'cos any whole or partial revelations on your part to third parties will be regarded as ultra vires and may result in a writ fer habeas corpus!

DAN

Sod me!

AURELIA

Fascinating, if I may so comment, how the natural rhythms of American speech are so redolent of the rhythms of Shakespeare's verse.

BONNY	(*pleased*) Say . . . glad you think so, honey . . . May I call you Dame?
AURELIA	Just Aurelia. Oh God I'm blushing! What is it about tonight. Everything suddenly seems new minted!
BONNY	We'll talk money later. I'm Bonny Lee, of Lee an' Lee, Billy's manager . . .
GUNTER	He needs a manager?
BONNY	That guy needs a manager to go to the john. Now what would you say, as bone fide experts, if I said to you that Billy's ancestor, Wilbur Shake . . . the genuine, bloodline, DNA-line, direct descendant, albeit illicit, of William Shakespeare, left behind a signed letter, spellin' out the clue to Billy's illustrious lineage?
GUNTER	What letter?
	(BONNY *takes a plastic wallet from her shoulder bag. In it is a single sheet letter.*)
BONNY	Tell 'em how you came by it, Billy . . .
BILLY	When granpappy died last year, they bulldozed away his shack in the Blue Ridge Mountains fer highway widenin'. But by the back porch they dug up an' ol' iron box which I had opened by an' ol' Amish locksmith. Inside was this here letter dated 1635!
GUNTER	Certainly looks like seventeenth century calligraphy.
BONNY	What's "calligraphy"?
DAN	(*now fascinated*) Handwriting.

BONNY   I know it's handwritin', ya Limey creep. But
                 is it worth more if it's calligraphy?

AURELIA   It's a poem!

BILLY   Took me a whole week ter figure it out. (*He
                 reads.*)

                 "Whoso Thou art, if kin Thou beest,
                 That onlie believe that which Thou seest,
                 And must have writ that which is spoke,
                 Thy true name find beneath the oak."

GUNTER   Signed . . . yes it is . . . "Wilbur".

AURELIA   Wilbur Shake, 1635! But was "Wilbur" a
                 name at that time? One for Professor Stick of
                 the Bristol Etymological Institute, wouldn't
                 you say?

GUNTER   Or Croon at Cardiff.

AURELIA   Or Diggle at Aberdeen.

GUNTER   (*disapproving*) Yes.

DAN   (*admiring the 'con'*) This is great! This is
                 better than "Hitler's diaries"!

BONNY   Someone git this Brit prick outer here! Tell
                 'em about the oak, Billy.

BILLY   "Thy true name find beneath the oak." Like
                 he wuz sayin, "find a four hundred year ol'
                 oak and dig. Where d'you start? Ain't no oaks
                 around where granpappy's shack was. Jus'
                 pines. Dug around a few ol' oaks in Virginia . . .
                 nuthin'. Then it come ter me. That oak ain't
                 in Virginia at all.

                 (*He pauses dramatically.*)

DAN   Alright . . . at this point one of us should say,
                 "You mean?" Okay I'll say it . . . You mean . . . ?"

BILLY   It's right here in Stratford! Shakespeare's oak
             . . . the one he sat under. And, maybe, Wilbur
             sat right there with him, feelin' the sacred
             wings of posey a-brushin' his infant cheeks.

AURELIA   Oh no, no, no! Dear me no! That oak is
             apocryphal!

BONNY   Okay . . . we'll hire a tree surgeon. So long as
             we find the proof . . . and Billy here is the
             bona fide inheritor of Shakespeare's estate.

GUNTER   What estate?

BONNY   Due to the supposed cessation of
             Shakespeare's family line, they ain't paid out
             no royalties fer that guy's plays in four
             hundred years! We is owed zillions!

DAN   Nice try. Really nice. Royalties stop fifty
             years after the death of the writer.

BONNY   Up your union . . . Jack! Bonny Lee of Lee
             and Lee Associates ain't bein' put off by
             details like death! That thar Shakespeare
             Company's gonna have to be re-named the
             Royalty Shakespeare Company when I an' my
             client git through. An' I want into movie fees,
             TV residuals an' every durned last bit o'
             merchandise with my client's ancestor's face
             on it from T-shirts to goddamn spittoons!

AURELIA   (*laughs*) Oh dear me! The RSC's in enough
             trouble!

BONNY   Not nearly enough your Dameship! (*She
             indicates* GUNTER.) You bona fides
             authenticate the letter an' what we find under
             that tree an' you'll have a cut of the action.
             Billy, tomorrow we find the tree.

BILLY   Already bin told how to git there, Bonny . . .
             an' it has to be now while the stars is shinin'.

(*He picks up his belongings.*)

Great Bear, lead me to where the spirit of my
great for-bear once inhabited a human body
an' walked this earth. Great, great, great,
great, great, great granpappy William, I'm a
comin' to yer!

DAN   I've got to be in on this! If only he could take
               'em to the cleaners! That'd teach 'em to turn
               down "Sewage"!

(*They exit purposefully.*)

BONNY   Hey! Billy! You stupid bum! I wanna be there
               when you find it. An' I can't go into no
               woods at night! Not in these boots. These
               ain't my walkin' boots. These are my struttin'
               boots! Damn! Damn!

GUNTER   Please . . . please. May I ask something? Was
               there anything else in the iron box?

BILLY   Oh, jus' papers.

AURELIA   Papers?

GUNTER   What kind of papers?

BONNY   Nuthin' useful. Looked like an ol' playscript
               called . . . what was it . . . yeh . . . Love's
               Labours Won . . .

GUNTER   Gott in Himmel!

AURELIA   Shakespeare's missing play! After Love's
               Labours Lost he wrote Love's Labours Won
               but no one's ever found it.

BONNY   No . . . couldn't have bin by Shakespeare.

GUNTER   Why not?

BONNY   Well, Shakespeare was a genius, right?

AURELIA   Right.

BONNY   Well I ain't no genius but even I know you don't spell the word "won" W-U-N-N-E! Billy wanted to keep it but I threw it out.

GUNTER   With the garbage?

BONNY   No! We got laws against that these days. I put it out separate . . . fer re-cyclin'. Billy! Don' make any decision till I git to yer!

(She exits. AURELIA *and* GUNTER *exchange looks of awestruck horror. The lights fade to black.)*

Scene Four

The wood near Stratford. Bright moonlight. Owls and night sounds. ZANA *discovered.*

ZANA   Mira! Mira! I've lost her again. Which way's the moon? I saw it just now through the branches. Ah there she is . . . the woman in the moon. Stay right there while I get my direction. This is the Queen of the Fairies telling you! Queens of Fairies always have a moon . . . *(She quotes from the Dream.)* "Therefore the moon, the governess of floods, pale in her anger . . . " Who's there? What's that? *(Listens.)* Mira? Will all you trees stand still! *(She's very nervous.)* Oh mother moon don't go. Such a sad face. Such a lop-sided, gaping, lost and lonely face. Are you getting married in the morning? Mira! I'll try this way . . .

(She exits left. Instantly WEBBO *pops up from behind a bush watching her go with awe.* WEBBO *is dressed "New Age" and wears crystals.)*

WEBBO   Your Majesty! Your Majesty! It must be her! I
               haven't seen her for two hundred years! The
               Queen of Night in all her spell-bound
               loveliness! Could it really be her? I'll put her
               to the test. First I'll make myself invisible. If
               she can see me then it's her! If not she's
               mortal.

               (WEBBO *squeezes her fists hard and strains.*)

               I haven't done this for ages. Have I gone yet?

               (MIRA *enters, searching and nervous.* WEBBO
               *crouches, suddenly caught out . . . but soon
               realises that* MIRA *can't see her.*)

MIRA   Zana! No one here.

WEBBO   She's mortal! (*Sits on her heels and stares in
               curiosity.*)

MIRA   I don't like this. I haven't been in a wood
               since the usual squalid incident at thirteen,
               with the delivery boy and his bike. What a
               tip! Old Grolsch bottles. 7-up tins. A
               smashed-up TV. Who'd smash a TV up in a
               wood? Maybe someone who couldn't stand
               repeats. Condoms. Fag ends. Bog paper. It's
               like Dan's place in Earl's Court.

               (*She picks up a leaflet.*)

               What's this?

               (WEBBO *examines her closely as she reads.*)

WEBBO   If she doesn't like my wood she can get out of
               it!

MIRA   (*reads*) "The Shakespeare Sensation! Visit
               this newly opened revolution in Shakespeare
               exhibitions. Living exhibits! You actually
               take part! Feel what it must have been like to

be stabbed behind the arras. Take Juliet's
poison . . . guaranteed non-toxic."

WEBBO   Maybe she's a back-packer who's lost her
back pack.

MIRA   (*thinks she hears something*) What? Must be
the fairies. If you're listening . . . bring Zana
to me. I can't go on! I'll have to rest.

(WEBBO *stares at her as* MIRA *sinks wearily to
the ground. Then at speed she spins out an
invisible thread into the wings . . . then
begins to pull it in again. A magic shimmer as*
ZANA *enters, pulled by the invisible line,
without realising it.*)

ZANA   There you are!

MIRA   Oh! I thought you were a spook!

ZANA   I think I am . . . I seem to walk the air . . .

MIRA   Oh don't!

WEBBO   Your Majesty!

ZANA   And hear faint voices . . .

MIRA   No!

WEBBO   Yes! She can't see me but she hears. Oh
Majesty!

MIRA   (*as* ZANA *listens*) Are you alright?

ZANA   (*snapping out of it*) Not really. I've dropped
my bloody bag somewhere. If I don't find it
I'll have to cancel all my plastic . . .

(*With a shimmer* WEBBO *dashes off the way*
ZANA *came in and swiftly reappears with the
bag. She places it at* ZANA's *feet.*)

I shouldn't have dragged you here . . .

MIRA   I came of my own free will . . .

ZANA   It's my mental disturbance, not yours . . .

MIRA   It's better than the usual row with Dan. (*Sees
        the bag.*) Is that it?

ZANA   Is that what?

MIRA   (*pointing*) Your bag.

ZANA   I must be going moon mad!

        (*As* MIRA *speaks the following,* ZANA *picks up
        the bag and looks at her reflection in the lid
        mirror.*)

MIRA   He's taking it out on me 'cos they won't do
        "Sewage".

ZANA   My face!

        (*Rapidly* WEBBO *fishes out a face pad.* ZANA
        takes it and uses it.)

MIRA   (*quoting*) "It's all backing up Councillor
        Grimble! We've got the entire contents of our
        S-bends blowing up in our faces!"

        (*As* ZANA *pops the face pad back,* WEBBO
        *hands her a lipstick. She uses it, then thinks
        "funny".*)

WEBBO   I'll make myself visible again . . .

ZANA   What was that?

MIRA   "It's all backing up Councillor Grimble . . . "

ZANA   No . . . a faint voice . . . (*She listens hard.*)

WEBBO   But as a precaution I'll use my cover story . . .
        I am not a fairy . . . I am a New Age traveller
        and my ambulance has broken down by the
        wood.

(*She clenches her fists and strains.* ZANA *is still looking about for the origin of the voice. So is* MIRA, *in sympathy. Suddenly they both see the now visible* WEBBO *at the same time. They scream and take some paces away.*)

Don't be afraid! I mean no harm. No harm at all your . . . (*She cuts this off short.*) . . . My name is Webbo and I'm a . . .

MIRA   (*cutting in*) Oh it's alright. She's a New Age traveller. I expect you're living in the wood are you?

WEBBO   (*surprised*) Yes.

MIRA   (*to a puzzled* ZANA) You can tell by the Afghan hat and crystals.

WEBBO   My ambulance is broken down in the woods. I think it needs a new alternator.

ZANA   Shame. Well if you could show us the way out we'd be very grateful.

WEBBO   Out of this wood do not desire to go . . .

ZANA   That's my line in the play. Have you seen me in it?

WEBBO   Your Majesty? (*She hasn't.*)

MIRA   You're here alone?

WEBBO   I had a man called Clunk but he left me . . . to get an alternator . . .

MIRA   Just now?

WEBBO   A month ago . . .

MIRA   Well we'll be okay with all your healing crystals. (*To* ZANA.) Are you into crystals?

ZANA   No . . .

(WEBBO *takes crystals on strings and puts them round their necks.*)

WEBBO   (*to* ZANA) There's Aquamarine for you . . . that calms the nerves. (*To* MIRA.) There's Chrysocolla for you, the woman's friend . . . good for pre-menstrual tension.

MIRA   Thanks.

WEBBO   Onyx for serenity, Moonstone and Lapis Lazuli for balance and psychic force. I'd give you Peridot for abundance but it fell off the chain.

ZANA   I can't take these . . .

MIRA   (*out of the corner of her mouth*) Take them. She'll be offended . . .

WEBBO   (*hearing this*) In creation, taking and giving are one, Your Majesty. (*Listening.*) Wait! (*She listens again.*) Men!

MIRA   How d'you know?

WEBBO   They vibrate differently.

ZANA   Certainly do!

             (*We hear* BILLY *and* DAN *approaching. To keep their spirits up they are singing a country rendering of Shakespeare's lyric, "You spotted snakes with double tongue, Thorny hedgehogs, be not seen; Newts and blind-worms do no wrong, etc . . . "*)

WEBBO   (*feeling the vibes*) They are benign . . .

MIRA   Wanna bet?

             (BILLY *and* DAN *enter, singing.*)

BOTH   "Come not near our Fairy Queen!"

DAN   (*seeing* WEBBO) Who's this?

WEBBO   I'm Webbo. My ambulance has broken down.

DAN   I know the feeling . . .

BILLY   Howdy, Mizz Webbo.

WEBBO   Ready!

     (*Her reply, a throw back to being a serving fairy to Titania puzzles them slightly. A short, sharp uncertain pause. Then* ZANA *breaks it.*)

ZANA   She lives in the wood . . .

BILLY   Then she'll know Shakespeare's oak . . .

WEBBO   Whose?

     (*Again, a brief hiccup. She's apparently never heard of him. They give up.*)

MIRA   (*to* DAN) I don't suppose you came because you were concerned about me?

DAN   Course I was. Out in the dear old country side full of psychopathic yokels with chain saws and rampant tribes of Visigoths gang-banging their way through the dreaming shires! Not that you wouldn't be more than a match for them.

MIRA   Drop dead!

     (*She turns her back on him. He's inwardly concerned . . . trapped in his own sarcasm.*)

BILLY   Mizz Zana, may I say how radiant you look by moonlight?

ZANA   And this is the man who doesn't come to see me?

BILLY   Oh what a rogue and peasant slave am I! But I see you now on God's own stage . . . under the whispering arch of his own showplace,

Mizz Zana. An' his silver spotlamp lights
your divine countenance, and all the leaves
flutter their applause.

(*Suddenly a commotion, as* BONNY *comes
breathlessly towards them. She enters.*)

BONNY   Billy! What you go so fast fer ya stupid punk!
I'm bein' follered! They're right behind!

BILLY   Who are, Bonny?

BONNY   Them!

BILLY   Which them?

BONNY   Them them! They're like breathin' an'
wheezin' an' hollerin'. Keep 'em away!

(*Everyone huddles together for safety.*)

BILLY   C'mon Bonny. Jes' someone out joggin'.

DAN   On four legs . . .

BONNY   It's them!

(AURELIA *and* GUNTER *arrive, breathing and
wheezing, fit to drop.*)

AURELIA   (*gasping*) We . . . we . . . must. . . speak to
you!

GUNTER   Bitte . . . moment bitte!

BONNY   Keep off! Bone fide experts! She was after
me! She probably got degrees in perversion!

AURELIA   No! (*Gasp.*) No! (*Gasp.*) English Literature!

GUNTER   Miss Lee . . .

BONNY   Keep away!

GUNTER   We had to ask you about Love's Labours Won . . .

AURELIA	Maybe you didn't put it out for recycling after all . . .
GUNTER	Think very carefully . . .
AURELIA	We appreciate your ecological intentions.
BONNY	Fergit that pile o' trash! It's probably been processed by now into somthin' really great . . . like a smash-hit Broadway musical!

(*Groans from* AURELIA *and* GUNTER.)

GUNTER	Maybe we could fax the garbage company?
BONNY	In the middle of a wood?
GUNTER	Oh . . . is this a wood? (*He looks about.*) Mein Gott! It's all trees!
BILLY	Never you mind about Love's Labours Won, your Dameness, I read it through a couple o' times and it's all right here in my li'l ol' head . . .
AURELIA	You have committed it to memory?
BILLY	Sure have . . .
GUNTER	Please! Please! Say some of it!
BILLY	Gee! Well . . . er . . . "Love's Labours Won . . . Actus Primus, Scene the First: Navarre. A garden near the palace. Enter Berone and Costard. Berone: "Costard speak! Is that the sharp-tongued Rosaline that spurs with pretty pricks across the park?"

(MIRA *is suddenly startled.*)

MIRA	What's that?
BONNY	That Love's Labours Won shit, honey . . .
MIRA	No. Not that! That shaking in the ground!

(*A low note of strange, deep tone.*)

WEBBO   It's a tree warning!

ZANA   What's a tree warning?

WEBBO   It travels from root to root, Your Majesty . . .

ZANA   Don't call me that — you're unsettling me . . .

DAN   A light!

MIRA   Where?

DAN   In the wood!

WEBBO   He's coming . . .

AURELIA   Oh God!

WEBBO   He's coming with green about him!

           (*The light now grows stronger and the sound
           takes on an eerie beat, louder and louder.
           WEBBO begins to sway and swoop around the
           stage.*)

           By the lay lines of earth . . . by the third eye
           and the seven Chakras of the body of the
           Goddess! He returns! Hide! Hide! In acorn
           cups! Flee, Your Majesty. Flee!

           (*In the blinding light and roaring sound
           everyone exits. Green smoke billows through
           the wood. Out of it emerges a shiny lizard-like
           man in greenish-black motorbike leathers and
           a blank, iridescent visored helmet. The figure
           removes the helmet. It is KOICHI. He looks
           about the empty clearing with ecstasy.*)

KOICHI   At last! I am here Master!

           Blackout.

ACT TWO

Scene One

The same, a moment later. KOICHI, *exactly as before, helmet in hand, addresses Shakespeare's spirit.* WEBBO *will creep back fearfully and hide.*

KOICHI   Master! Poet of poets. Mind of minds. The woodland was always the true centre of your soul . . . Japan salutes you. I salute you, as do all hidden creatures of unseen, unseeable power. Let time be meaningless. Age and years an illusion. The young are older than they seem . . . the old, reborn. For all of us are one in you, sweet swan of Avon.

          (RAFE *enters, also in biker gear but a baggier version. He carries a crash helmet.*)

RAFE   Koichi! Brilliant! Brilliant! What a ride. White knuckle all the way.

KOICHI   I was once the cross-country motorcycle champion of Osaka.

RAFE   When you took to the fields I closed my eyes. When I opened them we seemed to be riding through the trees . . . I mean, literally, through them!

KOICHI   It seems like that first time. (*He 'sees' without looking around.*) Who is it?

          (WEBBO *emerges, nervously.*)

WEBBO   I am Webbo . . .

RAFE   What are you doing here?

WEBBO   I'm a New Age traveller and my ambulance . . . (*Weakening under* KOICHI'S *gaze.*) . . . has broken down . . .

KOICHI	Then we must see it mended.
WEBBO	(*entranced*) Yes . . .

(RAFE *is caught up in the spooky atmosphere without knowing what goes on.*)

RAFE	So. Well. Brilliant! Where are they? Have you seen anyone in the wood?
KOICHI	We seek Titania. This is Oberon.
WEBBO	Yes, your Majesty . . .
RAFE	(*with an uncertain laugh*) Ha, ha, ha! Have you seen her?
WEBBO	They are wandering round and round and round and round . . .
RAFE	In circles?
WEBBO	In ellipses. People think they go round in circles when they're lost. But seen from above they go in ellipses.

(RAFE, *mentally agitated, does not see the implications of this.*)

RAFE	Poor Zana! You stay here. Don't move. I'll do a . . . an ellipse.

(*He sits.*)

KOICHI	How now, spirit?
WEBBO	I'm not a spirit. I'm a New Ager. Down with mortgages and income tax . . . up with psychic energy and higher being!
KOICHI	(*slightly insistent*) You are a spirit.
WEBBO	I'm not! (*Nervous.*) But I know you are.

KOICHI (*grins*) Whither wander you?

WEBBO Oh, here and there. You know . . . up and down . . . and things. (*Furiously, aside.*) I must not rhyme . . . I must not rhyme!

KOICHI Whither wander you?

WEBBO (*unstoppably*)
By Stonehenge and Glastonbury,
Hadrian's Wall from sea to sea.
By motorways where hawks do hover,
And little by-ways we discover.
Commons disappearing fast,
Scraps of wood that will not last.
In vans and buses full of tat,
Over hedgehogs all squashed flat,
To ancient, unknown holy places,
Where old magic leaves its traces.
In summer bean fields dancing jigs,
Battling with the blue-arsed pigs,
And into prison cell so bare . . .
Oh we do wander everywhere!

(*She finishes, knowing she's rumbled.*)

I've given myself away haven't I? I couldn't stop rhyming . . . Why are you here?

KOICHI To commune with the spirit of Shakespeare.

WEBBO I think you're here for their wedding . . . which may not now take place. Help her! Help my Queen! She's turning herself against it . . . I know she is.

KOICHI There is a moon above us and warm midsummer night to caress the heart. She will change her mind.

WEBBO No. The hemispheres of her mind are unbalanced and she is full of negativity . . . help her! For if they do not marry, who will marry? They'll undo the earth and who will

heal it then? You see how we are now!
Divided! Dying! Help her . . .

KOICHI   Yes I can do it . . . with old charms in a new
guise. You have your mortal alias . . . I have
mine. I am senior sales executive of Toshara,
the great Japanese pharmaceutical company. I
am here in England to plan the test marketing
of this small tablet with revolutionary
properties.

(*He unzips his top and takes a small plastic
tablet dispenser from his inside pocket. He
shakes one on to his hand.*)

WEBBO   What does it do?

KOICHI   It makes people well-disposed towards people.

WEBBO   (*holding her hand over it to 'feel' its
properties*) It's a love potion!

KOICHI   Don't say that. If the British Department of
Trade suspect that they will remove our
licence! We call it Amico . . . the friendly
tablet for everyone. You take one before
meeting bank manager. School-teacher takes
one before meeting class. But if taken in the
moonlight . . . who can say?

WEBBO   I know the flower you made it from . . .

KOICHI   Sssh! I will give one to your Queen when the
first person she sees after will be Mr Duke.

WEBBO   But she'll know . . .

KOICHI   I have coffee in the saddle bag of my Suzuki.
Wait!

(*He exits.*)

WEBBO   Can I trust him? I don't know . . . but he's all
the help I can get.

RAFE	(*off*) Zana!
WEBBO	Here, Your Majesty!
	(RAFE *enters*.)
RAFE	Here? What d'you mean? Where is she?
WEBBO	She'll be here soon . . .
	(KOICHI *re-enters, carrying a large flask of coffee and plastic cups*.)
KOICHI	I bring coffee.
RAFE	She'll drive me mad!
	(WEBBO *quickly spins out her 'line' to off-stage*.)
	I've angered her, I know. This wedding! I wanted it to say how much I valued her. Or did I want it to show her off to the world . . . to say, "look what I've captured?"
	(*Now* WEBBO *is pulling in her line, trying not to let him see her doing it. He does, however. She freezes as she realises that* RAFE *is watching her in astonishment*.)
	What are you doing?
KOICHI	They are Japanese exercises I have been teaching her.
	(WEBBO *continues to pull on the 'line' but in a more oriental fashion. Soon* ZANA *is 'pulled' on to the stage*.)
ZANA	Who's there? Who is it? Where is this?
RAFE	It's me, my love! Don't be afraid!
ZANA	You! Oh God, you've followed me. I said we were to go our separate ways for one night . . . just one night!

RAFE   I was worried about you . . .

            (*He tries to embrace her but she pulls back.*)

ZANA   So am I. I'm worried about me . . . that's why
            I'm here! To be with myself and think . . .

RAFE   But half of Stratford's here!

ZANA   Don't I know it! No offence to you Koichi . . .
            or to you Webbo . . . but I have to have a
            little space now. (*To* RAFE.) And you
            shouldn't have followed me!

RAFE   Zana . . . it's tomorrow . . . I have to have
            some certainty . . .

ZANA   Oh do you? Then it's your fault you asked too
            soon. (*She takes off her ring.*) Do you see this
            nice, old fashioned, traditional diamond ring?
            Take a close look. A symbol. Love needs no
            symbols.

            (*She holds it out to him.*)

WEBBO   (*aside to* KOICHI) Quick! The tablet!

            (KOICHI *deftly pops a tablet into a plastic cup
            of coffee.*)

ZANA   It's yours, Rafe . . .

KOICHI   Coffee?

ZANA   (*ignoring him*) Take it.

WEBBO   Your Majesty! Diamond is the sovereign of
            healing crystals removing all barriers to
            serenity.

ZANA   In that case you had better have it back.

RAFE   Don't do this!

WEBBO   Don't! Don't!

ZANA   (*to* WEBBO) Will you keep out of this! Rafe, there's no more to say. Apologise to the guests for me . . . and the critics.

RAFE   I'll stop the reception. I'll cancel all the invitations . . . only marry me!

ZANA   (*touched*) That would be a loving thing to do, Rafe. Let me know when you've done it . . . then we'll talk.

(*As she goes* KOICHI *again offers the coffee.*)

No! I don't want a coffee!

(ZANA *exits, half at war with herself.*)

RAFE   I despair. I despair. Do I deserve all this grief? Yes. Out of my love for her I've overdone it all! But . . . surely she could have played it as a part?

WEBBO   Her higher consciousness will not allow her to . . .

RAFE   I can't see which way to go . . . I don't need a wood to be lost in. I'm lost in my own head . . .

KOICHI   It only seems so. These are the small hours when the spirit is at its lowest ebb. The darkness of the morning has risen to meet his brother, the darkness of the night. They are as two black silk scarves drawn one across the other, so where they overlap the shadows deepen . . . but soon will pass.

(RAFE *slumps in despair.*)

WEBBO   We must find her and persuade her.

KOICHI   Have no fear Mr Duke. She shall come to you here . . . on this spot.

(*They exit.*)

RAFE

Get a hold on yourself. Look at it squarely.
Cancel. How? Can't make a hundred and fifty
phone calls. The cars. Oh God . . . the
marquee! It's there. They've pitched it. What
do I do? Ring the scouts and say d'you want a
big tent for the night? And could you use five
thousand vol-au-vents and some crates of
champagne? I'm right in the mire whatever I
do.

(BILLY *enters, cautiously.*)

BILLY

Well am I glad to meet someone. Mr Duke,
I'm fair tuckered tryin' ter figure which way
ter go . . . what with the heat an' all . . . and
the skeeters!You'd think you was in the
Everglades, not li'l ol' England.

(*He smacks away an insect.*)

RAFE

She won't marry me, Billy . . .

BILLY

You're speakin' of the Queen of the Night,
ain't yer?

RAFE

I can't believe she's said it . . .

BILLY

You sure are a lucky guy, Mr Duke . . .

RAFE

Lucky? The caterers are going to have me for
breakfast!

BILLY

She's a wonderful woman. Ain't never seen a
female more with such grace. I mean there's
Bonny, struts like a hobbled chicken . . . but
Zana don't even walk . . . she glides!

RAFE

I'm talking to myself here.

BILLY

Sir, if I got to the end of the rainbow . . .
wouldn't need no pot o' gold . . . providin' at
the end of it there was a woman as fine as
your Mizz Zana.

RAFE

(*bitter*) Thanks for making me feel better . . .

(*He begins to get out of the motorbike gear.*)

BILLY   You know . . . I reckon I've got jet-lag. I
mean you don' know what day of the week it
is when you're up in the stars eatin' lunch at
three in the mornin' and throwin' back the
liquor as you fly into the dawn . . .

RAFE   Where are they? What are they doing?

BILLY   (*noticing the gear*) Hey . . . you came here on a
motorcycle? That's what all the roarin' was . . .

RAFE   Koichi brought me on his Suzuki.

BILLY   Which model?

RAFE   I'm sorry . . . I don't know about those things.
He calls it "the Supernatural" . . .

BILLY   Suzuki Supernatural . . . Don't reckon I heard
o' that one. Always promised myself a
motorbicycle. Maybe a Harley Davidson, ye
know? Ever see Jack Nicholson in 'Easy
Rider'? (*Picks up the helmet.*) Got this
American football helmet on his head. Says,
"Man! Have I got a helmet!" An' he does that
ol' Jack Nicholson smile . . . like this . . .

(*He does his Jack Nicholson smile.* RAFE
decides he can't stand any more.)

RAFE   If anyone comes I've gone . . . Unless it's her
in which case I've gone to look for her . . .

(*He exits, having puzzled himself by this last
piece of information.*)

BILLY   Just be real nice to git that throttle in yer
hand. (*He does a bike engine.*) Brrrrrr!
Yeeeeaaaagh! (*He looks round fuzzily.*) Mr
Duke! Must have gone fer a piss. Wonder if
he'd mind me tryin' this on fer size?

(He puts on the bike overalls then holds the helmet over his head.)

Yup! "Man! Have I got a helmet!"

(BILLY *lowers the helmet. It's a tight fit.*)

Hey . . . gotta work a little here . . . that's it. *(The helmet now in place, he makes more engine noises.)* Raaaaah! Raaaaah! Nyeeeeeaaaaaaah!

(As he takes a bend he lurches a bit.)

Gee! That 747's got to me. I got jet-lag on my jet-lag. Hey, I'm bushed! Jes' close my eyes a while . . .

(He tries to get the helmet off. It won't co-operate.)

Won't come past my ears! No sense in pullin' 'em off . . .

(He curls up on the ground with the helmet and overalls on.)

Kinda cosy in here. An' it keeps out the skeeters! Goodnight England. Goodnight Stratford upon the Avon. Tomorrow we'll find ourselves that oak . . . that oak tree . . . sure will . . .

(He lowers the visor of the helmet and goes to sleep. Drowsy music. Through it we hear voices of the others, lost in the wood.)

BONNY	*(off, very distant)* Billy . . . Billy! Where is you, Billy?
A WHISPER	*(over speakers, very close)* Sleep, Billy . . . sleeeeep, Billy Shake . . .
RAFE	*(off)* Let's talk about it, Zana! Zana! Listen!

MIRA   (*off*) Dan . . . Dan . . . I'm sick of this wood.
                Dan!

DAN   (*further off*) Mira! Mira! I'm with Bonny . . .
                I'm with Bonny . . . I'm with Bonny!

GUNTER   (*distant*) Aurelia! Aurelia!

AURELIA   (*nearer, then further*) Is it you, Gunter . . . Is
                it you?

                (*The voices overlap with the music and make
                a swaying lullaby.* KOICHI *enters, still with the
                coffee.*)

KOICHI   We have found your lady Mr Duke, dropping
                sad petals in a still green pool and adding to
                its waters with her tears . . . Mr Duke!

                (*He pauses, realising "Mr Duke" is asleep,
                not realising it's* BILLY *in the biker gear.*
                WEBBO *enters, leading* ZANA *by the hand.*)

                Ssh! He sleeps . . .

ZANA   (*turning to go*) Then we won't wake him . . .

WEBBO   No you must stay and sooth his dreams. He
                might be having nightmares. I will read them
                for you . . .

                (BILLY *turns in his sleep.* WEBBO, *thinking
                he's* RAFE, *puts a hand above the helmet to
                receive the vibes.*)

                (*surprised*) Oh! It's not very clear but he
                seems to be in an aircraft playing cards.
                People are bringing him sacks of money . . .

ZANA   (*pleased*) Maybe he's going to get a TV
                series! Let's leave him to it.

WEBBO   No . . . sit by him please. And when he wakes
                he'll find you there, smiling forgiveness, your
                astral being perfectly centred.

ZANA   (*humouring her*) Right.

                   (*She sits not far from the sleeping* BILLY.
                   KOICHI *hands her the coffee when* WEBBO
                   nudges him and ZANA *takes it absently.*)

WEBBO   We'll go now, your Majesty.

ZANA   (*absently*) Right . . . (*Sighs.*)

                   (WEBBO *and* KOICHI *hide behind a bush.*)

                   Maybe, in wantin' this wedding, he's only
                   giving way to an understandable reaction.
                   You see, for thousands of years men have
                   found marriage a barrier to their true desires.
                   (*Imitates.*) "Come on let's play, hey? Sleep
                   with me, sleep with me, sleep with me." But
                   the barrier stayed put . . . with a few
                   exceptions like Samoa and the Trobriand
                   Islands . . . and Basildon. Then, for the first
                   time in recorded history, women began to say,
                   "Okay. Doors open. Bed's made. Jump in.
                   Bring your own soap, towel and dental floss."
                   At first the men couldn't believe it. "Hey,
                   hey, hey!" But then they thought, "Funny."
                   And after a while it was, "Am I being used
                   here or what?" And they'd dream of the days
                   when women were men's property and you
                   could take one home like a microwave or a
                   scuba diving set . . . and have your own neat
                   little guarantee. So, suddenly, marriage, the
                   old barrier, becomes the seal on a "lasting and
                   loving relationship" . . . especially now you
                   don't get separate tax allowances on
                   mortgages.

                   (*Deeply lost in thought,* ZANA *drinks the
                   coffee.*)

WEBBO   (*whispers*) At last! Now let your nuptials draw
                   near . . .

ZANA	(*to herself*) No! I'm not going to go through with it. (*She drinks again.*) I'll go before he wakes up. (*Finishes the coffee, while* WEBBO *and* KOICHI *watch for results.*) Sleep sound.
	(ZANA *gets up.* WEBBO *and* KOICHI *duck down. As she goes to exit,* ZANA *suddenly stops in her tracks. Her hormones begin to stir.*)
	Oooops! What's this? Oh not now! For heaven's sake woman. Get a hold of . . . Rafey? You awake?
	(*She slowly begins retracing her steps.*)
WEBBO	We'll leave her . . .
KOICHI	One moment. Interesting clinical test . . .
WEBBO	You knavish sprite! You're not just the cross-country champion of Osaka . . . you are a bit of a larker. Now let your tablet do more good to other lovers in this wood. (*Irritated.*) I must stop rhyming!
	(*She leads* KOICHI *away.* ZANA *enfolds the supposed* RAFE *in her arms and unzips his overalls, slipping a hand inside.*)
ZANA	Zippie, zippie, zippie . . . anyone at home?
	(BILLY *lifts his visor.*)
BILLY	Gee! Is this jet-lag?
ZANA	(*lovingly*) Why . . . you're not Rafe at all . . . you're Billy!
BILLY	Sure am . . . ma'am. I'll go get Rafe . . .
ZANA	Never mind Rafe. Let him stew . . .
BILLY	Oooh. Kinda got cramp somewhere . . .
ZANA	Take off your helmet . . .

BILLY	Now there I got a problem, Mizz Zana . . . Can't seem ter git it off.
ZANA	I'll get it off!
	(*She heaves at the helmet.* BILLY *hollers inside it. After a struggle, it finally comes free.*)
BILLY	Wow! Think my ears is stopped workin' . . .
ZANA	Billy . . .
BILLY	Yes ma'am . . .
ZANA	You won't need your ears.
BILLY	No ma'am.
	(*Blackout.*)

Scene Two

Another part of the wood. BONNY *and* DAN *enter, with* MIRA *following.*

BONNY	Ya dumb Limey bum! We passed this same spot three times already!
DAN	No we haven't.
BONNY	I swear by the knothole on that tree.
DAN	Twice then. We've got to be getting nearer the edge of the wood. The rubbish is increasing.
BONNY	Only the kind you is talkin' honey.
MIRA	Oh shut up quarrelling. Let's use our heads.
BONNY	Okay Superwoman. Let's have the benefit of your mental print-out.

MIRA	Get lost!
BONNY	I am lost.
MIRA	Just shut up, stand still and think.
	(*Pause.*)
	I mean where's the North Star?
DAN	West London. It's a pub in Ealing.
BONNY	You're kinda cheap, ain't yer?
DAN	I was trying to cheer us up.
BONNY	Oh, don't give me that plucky Falkland Island spirit . . .
MIRA	I'm going . . .
BONNY	The only place you goddamn Brits is goin' is downhill fast!
MIRA	Dan. Let's go.
DAN	You said stop and think.
MIRA	I can't with Colonel Sanders' finger lickin' friggin' daughter rabbiting on and on, can I!
BONNY	You Brit bitch!
MIRA	Yankee slag!
BONNY	Here . . . Who're you a-callin' a Yankee?
	(MIRA *explodes and exits. A pause.*)
DAN	Mira! Come back! If we have to resort to cannibalism I want you, not her! (*Indicating* BONNY.)
BONNY	Jeez . . . A whole two hours without room service!
	(KOICHI *enters, with two coffees.*)

KOICHI	I brought a thermos. Thought you might like some coffee.
DAN	You genius!
KOICHI	No . . . I am not a genius. But I know a man who was. Miss Lee . . .

(*He offers it, but she refuses.*)

BONNY	Ain't drinkin' Brit coffee. Good coffee in Britland is as rare as a dry martini in Salt Lake City.
KOICHI	This is made the Japanese way.
BONNY	You don't fool me. Japan's jes' another dumb tea drinkin' country an' you know it.
DAN	(*calling*) Mira! Coffee!
BONNY	She's walked out on yer an' it don't surprise me none. Why any able-bodied female stays in this un-sceptred isle with you race of second-rate has-bins is well beyond the comprehension of the lowest critter in creation.
DAN	You are puke personified.
BONNY	Yeh!
DAN	Get back to the United Shites . . .
BONNY	Yeh?
DAN	Numero uno superpower! All you are these days is a gas-guzzling, junk food eating, junk culture spreading, junk nation living off junk bonds!

(*He takes a swig of coffee as* WEBBO *enters.*)

BONNY	C'mon, drool Britannia . . . Let's hear it, boy!

DAN You've gone . . . (*He falters.*) You've gone.
(*He looks at her with a new and growing
interest.*) You've gone all misty. (*He gives
her a dreamy, loving look.*)

BONNY I've what?

DAN Like those movie close-ups where they smear
vaseline round the lens . . . and a woman
becomes an etherial vision . . . no longer of
this world.

WEBBO (*aside to* KOICHI) It's the wrong one!

KOICHI (*showing the tablet dispenser*) No. Amico. In
the coffee . . .

(*He demonstrates by shaking another in the
coffee he's holding.*)

DAN (*to* BONNY) You're beautiful!

WEBBO (*aside to* KOICHI) I mean the wrong lover!

BONNY What's this guy gittin' at? Maybe I do need that
coffee . . .

(*She takes it like a restorative in one gulp.*)

DAN I spoke such harsh and hateful words to you
Miss Lee. Can you find it in your heart to
forget them and begin afresh?

BONNY All you'll git from me is my . . . (*The tablet
begins to work.*) . . . My . . . My . . . Oh my!
Dear Daniel, how I've misjudged you. It's
like the pages of our story have been blown
by a great wind . . . and suddenly they've
stopped at a new and truthful portrait of you.
Why sir . . . I see a glint in your eye I never
saw before . . . of tenderness . . . and
experience.

(*They embrace.*)

KOICHI   Will that be all?

BONNY   GIT!

WEBBO   (*looking with disdain at a grinning* KOICHI) I
              should have known!

              (*They find a hiding place to observe.*)

DAN   Have you ever looked at Emily Bronte?

BONNY   Never mind Emily Bronte! Come, let us find a
              more private place than this, where prying
              eyes cannot behold our bliss!

              (*As they go to exit,* MIRA *enters.*)

MIRA   What's this? You toerag! I leave you two
              minutes! Two minutes! And suddenly it's
              Rhett Butler and Scarlet! You've been having
              me on! It was phoney war to my face . . . and
              this behind my back!

DAN   I hope you are going to be adult about this.

BONNY   I'm sorry honey. I really am, but . . .

MIRA   (*to* DAN) Take your hands off that woman's
              body!

DAN   (*to* BONNY) Excuse me, Miss Lee. She appears
              to be one of the common sort . . .

              (*He takes* MIRA *a little aside.*)

              F-off! Go home. Wash your hair. Watch late
              night TV. Ring your agent!

              (*He returns to* BONNY.)

BONNY   We don't wanna hurt no one, honey. We . . .
              well . . . we jus' need one another so much!

              (*They exit.* WEBBO *and* KOICHI *observe.*)

WEBBO	(*aside*) Can't you reverse it?
KOICHI	You cannot take aspirin and have your headache back. But . . . I shall make one for her. (*He does so.*)
MIRA	There's something strange going on. Is it a trick? Is Dan just winding me up? But people go mad in woods, I've read about it. Maybe something came out of the shadows and possessed them. A sort of Dionysian urge. A mass hysteria . . . for two . . . (RAFE *enters.*)
RAFE	Ah . . . you're Mira.
MIRA	That's right.
RAFE	Terrific talent. Stay with it! Make the breaks!
MIRA	Yes. Fine.
RAFE	Have you seen Koichi or Webbo?
MIRA	They're somewhere near. Have you seen Dan?
RAFE	I have, yes . . . (*Wonderingly.*) With . . . how shall I describe her?
MIRA	Take your time.
RAFE	I mean . . . are they going swimming? (MIRA *exits fast.* KOICHI *and* WEBBO *emerge.* KOICHI *is still holding the 'laced' coffee for* MIRA.)
WEBBO	Has she changed her mind, Your Majesty?
RAFE	I don't know. I haven't found her yet. Have you?
KOICHI	We brought her to you . . .
RAFE	Where?

WEBBO	Where we left you, Your Majesty!
RAFE	And now she'll be there wondering where I am.
KOICHI	But you were there!
RAFE	I know. Stupid, isn't it? Thanks.

(*Before they can prevent him he has taken the coffee from* KOICHI, *thinking it is on offer. He takes a sip. At the same moment* AURELIA *enters with* GUNTER *a little behind.*)

AURELIA   (*absorbed in her theme, to* GUNTER) . . . so you see the real nub of the problem is going to be the total lack of documentary evidence. I mean to have the text of Shakespeare's lost play, *Love's Labours Won*, only available through the head of a decidedly unacademic, if rather jolly, Country and Western singer may not have sufficient credibility. However, never let it be said that lack of solid evidence ever deterred the true Shakespearean scholar.

(*Throughout this* RAFE *has been subjecting* AURELIA *to an increasingly amorous regard.*)

RAFE   Aurelia . . .

AURELIA   Oh hello! You're Rafe Duke.

RAFE   Aurelia . . .

AURELIA   Yes, that's little me. Gunter . . . Rafe Duke, our splendid Oberon . . .

(*As a stupefied* GUNTER *puts out his hand* RAFE *puts the cup with the rest of the coffee in his hand . . . then takes* AURELIA'S *arm.*)

RAFE   We must talk . . .

AURELIA   Oh yes we had a rather chirpy conversation at that reception for the Council to meet the actors. Your cocktail onion fell in my punch.

RAFE   I know a bank where the wild thyme grows . . .

AURELIA   Why that's . . . that's . . . (*She is about to say, "That's Oberon's speech".*)

RAFE   I'll take you there . . .

AURELIA   How interesting . . . (*Rummaging.*) I think I've got my diary here somewhere.

RAFE   Our bed I'll make of musk rose and eglantine . . .

AURELIA   Gunter . . . (*She has made her decision.*)

GUNTER   (*still warily mesmerised by* RAFE'S *transformation*) Ja?

AURELIA   I'll just take a quick peek. It's the Wild Thyme I can't resist . . .

(RAFE *leads her away.*)

WEBBO   Oh no! No!

KOICHI   Excellent test results. I must contact Tokyo . . .

(*He takes out a state-of-the-art portable phone and dials.*)

GUNTER   (*still in shock*) I can't believe this is happening . . .

KOICHI   (*on phone*) Moshi, moshi. Koichi-desu. Hai! Testo wa umaku itemasu. (*Hello, hello. Koichi here. Yes! The test is going well.*) Subarashu! Hai . . . dewa kayoubi ui Aimashou! (*Excellent! Yes . . . see you on Tuesday!*)

GUNTER   I come to England to renew the love of my
              youth and she is taken from under my nose by
              a man half my age. Was the dream too
              perfect? Love is the rainbow that cannot last . . .

              (*He sees he is holding the coffee. He downs
              it.*)

WEBBO   Stop him! He's drinking it!

              (*But it's too late.* WEBBO *dives for cover
              behind* KOICHI.)

GUNTER   Nice coffee . . .

KOICHI   (*nervous*) Thank you.

GUNTER   Very nice . . .

KOICHI   Thank you.

GUNTER   Quite superlative. Did you make it yourself?

KOICHI   No . . . I confess, it was my hotel.

GUNTER   (*smiles*) Hmmm.

KOICHI   (*smiles*) Armmm.

GUNTER   Which is your hotel?

KOICHI   Ah . . . it is written down somewhere . . . I
              forget.

GUNTER   Could I ask you something?

KOICHI   Yes?

GUNTER   Do you like flowers?

KOICHI   (*hesitant*) Yes . . . I like flowers.

GUNTER   Shall we pick some?

KOICHI   Well . . . perhaps I don't like flowers as much
              as all that . . .

(GUNTER *begins to sing an old sentimental
Berlin cafe song from the 1920's.*)

GUNTER   Liebling mein Herz dich grüssen
          Nur mit Dir allein, kann es glücklich sein . . .

          (*As he sings he advances slowly towards*
          KOICHI *who stands rooted to the spot.* WEBBO
          gives him a "serves you right" look as GUNTER
          leads him gently off-stage.)

WEBBO   (*to the audience*) If he's with he . . .
          And he's with she . . .
          And Dan's with Bonny, as we've seen . . .
          That leaves one possibility,
          (*Horror.*) And he is with my Fairy Queen!

          (*Lights fade to black.*)

                     Scene Three

The first part of the wood where we left BILLY *and* ZANA. *He
is out of the overalls and his trousers. She is in her slip. Both
are garlanded with leaves and flowers.* BILLY *is telling her
his life story, his head in her lap.*

BILLY   . . . so I'd be about ten or eleven years of age
          when my granpappy comes a visitin', gits out
          his geetar an' I sing along with him. An' he
          says, "Billy, you goin' ter be a singer jes' like
          me. Gee, Mizz Zana . . . I must be borin' the
          pants off you . . .

ZANA   Tell me more. Tell me more and I will wind
          these midnight flowers about your head. Tell
          me everything!

BILLY   Well . . . my granpappy, Ben Shake . . .
          Mountain Ben, they called him, he takes me
          to hear all the bluegrass cats in town . . .
          Loretta Lynn, Billy Joe Shaver, Willie Nelson
          . . . an' I git to dream o' bein' up there meself.

ZANA   Which you did . . . in Nashville. Tell me
              about Nashville . . .

BILLY   Well . . . there was this ol' blues singer called
              Swamp Fever Pete. He says to me, Billy . . .

              (ZANA *hears something.*)

ZANA   Ssssh!

              (*Faintly, we hear* BONNY *and* DAN *singing a
              sweet Tennessee love song. It gets nearer.*)

              Bonny?

BILLY   Sure is, Mizz Zana . . .

              (*He gets up in haste.*)

ZANA   But it's me you love, Billy . . .

BILLY   Well now . . . sure has been nice knowin' you
              an' all, Mizz Zana. Apologies fer the jet-lag . . .

              (ZANA *kisses him.*)

              But . . . but if Bonny finds me with you I
              reckon I'm gonna be served up barbecued
              with smoked hickory sauce!

ZANA   Oh she shall not my love devour. Come! We
              will seek another bower . . .

              (ZANA *leads* BILLY *away, taking their clothes
              with them.* BONNY *enters, finishing her song.
              She carries her boots and jacket. Her shirt is
              open. There is pond weed in her hair.* DAN,
              *similarly half clad and barefoot, is looking
              pleased with himself.*)

BONNY   How d'you feel, boy?

DAN   Quite well really.

BONNY   Any complaints?

DAN	Er . . . no. (*Wonderingly*.) I can't think of a thing to say against it.

(MIRA *enters*.)

MIRA	Well I can!
BONNY	Honey, will you quit follerin'!
MIRA	I'm not following. I'm going the same way.
BONNY	Won't do you no good. By all o' cupid's goddamn arrows he's mine. Be a woman. Take it on the chin! He's coming with me ter Tennessee . . .and there a gracious room I shall design fer him . . . mahogany desks and shelves . . . quill pens an' quaint ol' ink wells. Damask cushions picked out with famous quotes. Portraits of the literary greats. The latest state-of-the-art word processor disguised as a Louis Quinze escritoire. An' there he'll write this Pulitzer Prize novel about a poor gel from Tennessee who has to claw her way to the top, who has ter fight fer everythin' she gits . . . an havin' gained success, finds there is a vacancy . . . a spiritual void in her soul which only he can fill.
MIRA	Well, from the author of "Sewage" that shouldn't constitute a major challenge.

(ZANA *re-enters, cautiously*.)

BONNY	Hi, honey! Can we help you?
ZANA	Erm . . . You haven't seen a pair of socks anywhere have you?
BONNY	If you mean Billy's they're right here. With his underpants.

(*She points them out sweetly.* BILLY *peeps in*.)

ZANA	Thank you.

BONNY   Glad to be of service. Hi, Billy.

MIRA   (*exploding with frustration*) What the effing
               hell is going on? Dan! Will you get your eyes
               focused? Snap out of it or I'll nail your
               gonads to that tree!

               (DAN *is uncharacteristically pained by this*.)

DAN   Please! Please! Why, why must we have all
               this gratuitous coarseness and violence? Our
               love is on a higher plane . . .

               (WEBBO *enters at speed*.)

WEBBO   Stop Your Majesty! Stop! It's all a terrible
               mistake! We meant to do good but Koichi
               kept mixing it all up. He has these tablets
               which make people well disposed towards
               people and he put one in your coffee, Your
               Majesty, which is all my fault because I
               thought if you did not marry the King of the
               Fairies the woods would shrink still further
               and more of the commons would disappear or
               be taken from us . . . the trees wither to sticks
               and the grass grow brown and dry! Hatred
               would rise . . . new strife break out and the
               world would sicken and die. Only your
               marriage could save us . . . but the tablet
               worked when you were with Billy and not the
               King - and the King went to look for you and
               he got a tablet intended for Mira but saw
               Aurelia just after Koichi had accidentally
               given one to Bonny and Dan.

MIRA   I knew there was a simple explanation!

ZANA   Webbo, I am not the Queen of the Fairies. I
               am simply the actress who plays her. I have
               no magic powers.

               (BILLY *clears his throat*.)

ZANA   Nothing of the supernatural about me . . .
                except your crystal. But, since these things
                are so important to you . . . and me . . . we
                must do our best to mend matters. Where's
                Koichi?

                (GUNTER *and* KOICHI *enter, arm in arm.*)

GUNTER   Ladies and gentlemen, Koichi and I have
                come out. Ah, if only this was Berlin in the
                twenties and you were Herr Issy-voo and I the
                handsome young German aristocrat, riding in my
                open landau to my palace in Charlottenburg . . .

KOICHI   In Japan love is a God. In the west love is a
                Goddess. Who cares?

MIRA   Koichi, this tablet. Isn't there an antidote?

KOICHI   My company is a responsible company. They
                did not wish to cause an epidemic of love.
                Otherwise managers might fall in love with
                staff . . . capitalist with trade unionist . . .
                people of one religious sect with those of
                another . . . nations we have only just heard
                of love other nations we had never heard of.
                Or police fall in love with New Age
                travellers. So we saw the vital need for an
                antidote.

MIRA   Where is it?

KOICHI   Unfortunately it has not yet been developed.

WEBBO   Then we must use the crystals . . .

                (*She takes them from a pouch, then hands
                them round.*)

                Azurite to cut through illusion; Celestite and
                Agate to reveal the truth. Emerald and Ruby
                for serenity; Onyx and Opal for self-esteem.
                But they are not enough. We must have
                Diamond, the greatest of the healers . . . I
                have none . . .

ZANA	I have. I gave it back to Rafe.
WEBBO	I'll bring him . . .
MIRA	How?
WEBBO	(*as she spins out her thread*) It's one of the few powers I still have. (*To* ZANA.) You say you're not the Queen . . . but you remember! My name is Webbo now, but you knew me long ago under a different name . . .
ZANA	(*the name comes to her*) Cobweb!
WEBBO	(*as she pulls in her line*) Cobweb!
	(*A shimmer as* RAFE *and* AURELIA *are drawn out of the wood and enter.*)
RAFE	And here they all are. Is it morning?
WEBBO	Almost, Your Majesty.
KOICHI	The morning of the moon will give way to the sun.
AURELIA	Oh this is terrible. You're all laughing at me! At first I thought I never looked for this love. It just found me. (*To* RAFE.) But then, as you lay sleeping, the wood seemed like a transparent box with us displayed to view. I couldn't hide my shame and humiliation. Oh why, as we get older, do we still have the ghost of youth inside us that never, ever leaves us alone!
RAFE	Why say these things? Love has no shame. Why should it? Nor has it any thought for age or years or time itself.
KOICHI	He's right. There's no law that says you must be young to love.
AURELIA	He doesn't mean it! He's an actor. He's acting a part. Gunter . . .

(GUNTER *links arms with* KOICHI.)

GUNTER   Please! I am not what I was!

WEBBO   Give me the diamond that is in your pocket,
           dread King of Shadows . . .

RAFE   (*takes out the ring*) This? No!

WEBBO   Quick! The night is ending!

RAFE   You shall not have it!

KOICHI   The lady, sir. She weeps in her soul. All must
           be mended. Even I, Koichi, secret trickster,
           elf, imp, crony of the Monkey King and
           general good fellow, say it should be done . . .

WEBBO   Please, Your Majesty . . .

           (RAFE, *reluctantly, hands over the diamond
           ring.* WEBBO *hands it to* KOICHI.)

           Hold it just above their heads. Eyes closed.

           (KOICHI *holds the ring over each person's
           head . . . where a halo might be on a saint. As
           he does so,* WEBBO *touches the forehead in the
           third eye position . . . centred between the
           eyes and a little above them.*)

           You will feel the diamond above you in the
           position of the first Chakra of the body. Let
           each mind reach up to the healer as I wake the
           third eye of self wisdom.

KOICHI   And as the earth spins eastward I call on
           Amaterasu, Goddess of the sun to send her
           first ray forth!

           (*A sun ray strikes the stage. Suddenly
           everyone feels their minds clearing.*)

ZANA   It's like a mist rising from your mind!

BILLY	Hey! Man! An' I didn't even take a tablet . . .
ZANA	Oh Billy! I'm sorry . . .
BILLY	(*aside*) I'm not . . . Your Majesty.
DAN	Whooooo! What's happening?
WEBBO	As the mind clears, the truth is revealed!
MIRA	(*to* DAN) How d'you feel?
DAN	Sort of decaffeinated. It wasn't me, Mira. If it had been me . . . really me . . . I'd have known where I belonged.
MIRA	Dan! I thought I was gettin' the thin end of this.
DAN	You are. (*They embrace.*)
BONNY	Billy! I see right through yer . . .
BILLY	You always did, Bonny!
BONNY	An' it's time you saw through me, ya dumb bum! I want your love . . . but instead of givin' it to me, you're jes' in love with the whole wide world, ain't yer? You gotter stop bein' so selfish!
RAFE	"Come my Queen, take hands with me And rock the ground whereon these sleepers be . . ."
ZANA	(*completing the quote*) "Now thou and I are new in amity."
GUNTER	Let me get this straight. Am I out of the closet or not?
AURELIA	Be interesting finding out won't it?
	(*She calls for silence.*)

Please everyone! Could I have your attention
for a tiny moment? I'm always having to
make speeches so I thought I'd make myself
useful after blubbing in that awful fashion.
'Nuff said about what took place last night.
The fling is flung, as it were. The thoughts we
are left with are our own. But it would be
remiss of me not to give thanks where thanks
is due. I propose a vote of thanks to Webbo!

(*Applause.*)

ZANA   Or should we say "Cobweb"?

AURELIA   Who?

ZANA   She's Cobweb. She's a spirit. I mean . . . she
                really *is* a spirit. A fairy!

AURELIA   Nonsense! There have been no authentic
                sightings of fairies in Warwickshire since
                1735!

DAN   If she's a fairy where's her wings?

WEBBO   I had 'em cut off. They get in the way in an
                ambulance. You can see the stumps if you
                want.

                (*Everyone gathers round to see.* WEBBO, *in
                front, lifts her T-shirt so they can see up it but
                the audience can't.*)

ALL   Yeeeeak!

DAN   Can you waggle them?

WEBBO   Yeh! (*She does so.*)

ALL   Yaaaaagh!

RAFE   Listen! Listen!

                (*We hear the dawn chorus. Sunlight streams
                down.*)

Dawn . . . and you may notice the suns' rays lighting the diamond on Zana's ring . . . now, once more, on her finger. Titania has consented to her wedding!

(*A cheer.*)

ZANA
With one condition. Before we go to Holy Trinity, I want a simple ceremony here. Simple vows, simply spoken without priest, choir or wedding march. A ceremony in our hands.

WEBBO
Oh, you could have the Scottish bucket wedding!

RAFE
What's that?

WEBBO
The bride pees in a bucket. The bridegroom pees in the same bucket. They swirl the pee around and the village elder says, "Whoever can separate these waters can separate this man and wife" . . . and he flings the pee high in the air! It makes me cry.

DAN
D'you have a bucket?

WEBBO
No.

ZANA
We'll save it for the steps of Holy Trinity. Everyone join hands. (*They do so.*)

RAFE
Make a circle around us.

(*Everyone forms a circle around* RAFE *and* ZANA.)

Zana . . . I marry you for life!

ZANA
Rafe . . . I marry you for life!

BILLY
Yee haw!

(*Applause and embracing.*)

KOICHI	Now you have the blessings of humans, the blessings of spirits and the blessings of William Shakespeare who once sat under this oak.

(He points upward into empty air.)

BONNY	Which oak? Where?
KOICHI	It stood right here on this spot.
BILLY	Shakespeare's oak? The oak I came to find?
KOICHI	Last winter they buzz sawed it down and took it away. A smart fellow who owns a chain of tourist shops bought it, cut it down to be split into ten centimetre pieces to be sold as souvenirs.
DAN	Hard luck, Billy.
BILLY	They dug up the roots an' all?
KOICHI	They were thorough, Mr Shake.
BONNY	You know . . . I'm sick of bein' an' entrepreneur.
WEBBO	It was huge and heavy with green. Spread out far and wide. To me it was a tree. All are sacred.
BILLY	*(quotes)* "Whoso thou are, if kin thou beest, That onlie believe that which thou seest, And must have writ that which is spoke, Thy true name find beneath the oak"
	Maybe it's sayin' Billy Shake is my true name!
BONNY	Right! An' it's a name anyone'd be proud to bear.
BILLY	Gee . . . Bonny!

(DAN *has found a piece of paper screwed up in the soil*.)

DAN   Billy! Look! A piece of paper!

MIRA   Give it him . . .

               (BILLY *smooths out the paper*.)

BILLY   It says, "Congratulations!" Hey now! (*He beams at everyone, then continues*.) "In a matter of days you could be on your way to winning one hundred thousand pounds in the incredible Shakespeare Sensation Grand Prize Draw!"

DAN   "You will be allocated six figures on our computer. Six lucky chances to win!"

BILLY   Reckon findin' I really was descended from the good William might have been more than I could handle . . . but I sure could handle a hundred grand!

RAFE   Now . . . you're all coming to the wedding.

BILLY   Comin' to it? Hey you cats! We is gonna' sing at it!

               (*Suddenly an army sergeant appears on night exercise, armed with an automatic weapon, face blacked. He is* SERGEANT 405.)

SGT 405   Alright, alright! Everyone relax. You are in the presence of the British Army, ladies and gentlemen, so no sudden movements, hands where I can see them and we'll all be good friends.

DAN   Who the hell are you?

SGT 405   Sergeant 405, special duties, night exercise. Are you aware that you are now in a restricted area?

MIRA	He's winding us up!
SGT 405	This wood is top secret.
RAFE	There were no notices . . .
SGT 405	You don't put up notices when it's secret.
AURELIA	Ridiculous! What's your name?
SGT 405	Sorry madam . . . that's secret too. But anyone who's anyone knows me as 405.
DAN	I thought we were having a more open society.
SGT 405	Oh we are, sir. Nowadays we readily admit we have secrets. We just don't tell you what they are.
AURELIA	You listen to me. I am a friend of the Lord Lieutenant of the county.
SGT 405	I'm glad about that, madam. He hasn't got many.
GUNTER	You are insulting this lady!
SGT 405	I'd insult you, sir, but I can't think what to say.
BILLY	Hi there . . .
BONNY	Billy . . . keep outer this . . .
BILLY	You must be quite familiar with the wildlife round here, Sergeant. Tell me, is that a robin on yonder bough?
SGT 405	No sir, it's an infra red surveillance camera. Now listen carefully. You have been closely observed during the night and your behaviour doesn't give you a leg to stand on. You have been seen imbibing illicit substances and

indulging in open air carnality . . . or as we
say, going at it like a garden gate. In other
words, banging in the wind. Would this by
any chance be an acid house party?

MIRA   No!

SGT 405   Pity. I've always wanted to be at one. I'm
              sorry but I shall have to hand you over to the
              civil authorities.

ZANA   Oh dear . . . and we were just about to leave.
              We had no intention of trespassing.

SGT 405   You're Zana Ferris! (*He is overcome with
              pleasure.*)

ZANA   Yes . . .

SGT 405   I saw you last Saturday matinee. A
              consummate performance if I may say so . . .

RAFE   I'm Rafe Duke . . .

SGT 405   Glad to meet you, sir. (*Then, ignoring him.*)
              Oh, your Titania was something miraculous,
              madam.

ZANA   Thank you!

RAFE   Yes, she was rather on song that matinee.
              Enjoy the play? (*He fishes for some
              recognition.*)

SGT 405   Quite a favourite with the troops. It's the
              fairies, you see . . .

WEBBO   The fairies?

SGT 405   Soldiers and fairies have a lot in common. We
              both mess about at night doing secret things
              in the woods . . . and you never really know
              whose side we're on. (*To* WEBBO, *sensing*

what she is.) We fixed your ambulance. It's
up on the road.

(WEBBO *is startled and very moved.*)

(*to* ZANA) So . . . these are all your friends are
they? Well I'll just set you on the way to
Stratford . . .

DAN   I still think this is a mad place to be doing
             military exercises . . .

SGT 405   Ah, that's the MOD in its wisdom, sir.
             Today's flash points are not only your deserts,
             jungles or far-off islands . . . no! Now it's
             your pretty little towns and villages nestling
             in green and pleasant valleys where the
             crunch is. Mind you, they don't need soldiers
             for that. If you want your house reduced to
             rubble, your wife raped and her and the kids
             made refugees you don't need soldiers to do
             it. Oh, no . . . your neighbour'll do that for
             you these days. Give him a second hand
             Kalashnikov and he's away. (*To* KOICHI.) That
             your motorbike, sir?

KOICHI   I shall remove it instantly.

SGT 405   Another fine day. I love these woods. They're
             magic!

             (THE SERGEANT *leads the way and all, save*
             KOICHI *and* WEBBO, *follow and exit.*)

WEBBO   He mended my ambulance. That's the first
             kindness any mortal has done me.

KOICHI   So maybe that makes you mortal. You cannot
             live a dream. The spirit world we knew will
             not return. He who sat beneath this invisible
             tree knew that well . . .

             (*The stage brightens with sunlight.*)

Amaterasu, the sun! Farewell Tsuki-Yoni, the
moon. In Japan we have no man in the moon
. . . and no woman. We have a rabbit . . .

(*He enjoys this thought.* WEBBO *weeps for the
spirit world gone. Fade to black.*)

Scene Four

*The wedding marquee, Stratford, later that day. Garlands
festoon the canvass. Champagne and food on a table.* BILLY *is
testing a microphone. A small combo of guitar, bass, drums,
if wanted. All the others are there except* WEBBO *and* KOICHI.
BILLY *calls singing instructions to* MIRA. [NB: *The dialogue
should be adapted to the way* BILLY *and* MIRA *will sing in the
final song.*]

BILLY   Okay, Mira. You got it?

MIRA   Think so. When you sing, "Ah . . . ah . . . ah",
               I sing, "Hey . . . hey . . . hey".

BILLY   One more time. "Ah . . . ah . . . ah".

MIRA   (*with him*) "Hey . . . hey . . . hey".

               (BONNY *has brought* AURELIA *alongside her.*)

BONNY   C'mon, your Dameship. You is gonna learn
               how ter strut. First position the chest . . . so.

AURELIA   You don't mean it . . .

BONNY   I do. Now the derriere . . . like so.

AURELIA   Like an S-bend?

MIRA   Don't mention S-bends. Makes me think of
               Sewage.

DAN   Alright . . . but you just think . . . that church
               today was teeming with directors. All on their
               knees! (*Savouring the thought.*) Putting the
               fear of God into God. Now . . . when one of
               them shows, what do you do?

MIRA	I do Sewage.
DAN	Good girl!
	(*She glugs champagne.* BONNY *inspects* AURELIA'S *struttin' position.*)
BONNY	Honey, you got more downstairs than that. Mind over body. You gotta think ass!
AURELIA	(*determined*) Ass! I suppose its like everything else in life, You have to keep things in balance.
BONNY	Jes' push it out till yer eyes pop! With the beat now. A doo . . . a doo . . . a doooo . . . doo . . . doo . . .
	(*They strut.* GUNTER *sidles up to* BILLY.)
GUNTER	Billy. I have made arrangements at the Institute to record you reciting the whole of Love's Labours Won. We must enshrine forever the world's greatest missing masterpiece!
BILLY	Funny you should say that, my friend . . . 'cos ever since Webbo purified my mind an' joined me to my higher brain function with that crystal therapy I can't recall a single word.
GUNTER	Nein! Schrecklich! You must remember!
BILLY	Nope. Clean an' serene.
GUNTER	You mean she wiped you?
BILLY	Guess so.
GUNTER	Where's Webbo?
DAN	Just getting her ambulance.
GUNTER	Good! She'll need it!

DAN	On the other hand, maybe she has a crystal for clogging up the mind with all the useless mental lumber you can't normally get rid of. Then it'll come back to him.
GUNTER	(*snatching at straws*) Possible . . . possible . . .

(*During this a character we haven't met before enters. This character, female or male, may or may not be the director* DAN *is anxious to meet. All she/he does is take a casual look around, pour some champagne, then listen embarrassed while* MIRA *blows her opportunity.*)

MIRA	(*swaying*) Who's that? . . .
DAN	(*uninterested*) God knows.
AURELIA	Seems vaguely familiar . . .
DAN	(*suddenly alert*) A director! Mira . . . a director!
MIRA	Where?
DAN	There! Come on . . . grab your opportunity . . .
MIRA	Sewage?
DAN	Sewage.
MIRA	I can't do it . . .
DAN	You can! (*To the stranger.*) I'm Dan Howard . . . "Gunge". I can see you're not the boring kind of person who thinks there's a time and place for everything. That's Mira Edge, brightest talent of her generation, and you will torture yourself with regret if you don't hear her right now. She's doing a piece from my latest play . . . "Sewage". Mira . . .

(MIRA *steadies herself and launches.*)

MIRA   "It's all backing up Councillor Grimble!
                We've got sewer rats in our S-Bends and old
                people blowing up in our faces! Look at it
                Councillor Grumble . . . Gumble . . . Gamble . . .
                an entire shitty up to its neck in cit!" Erm . . .

                (*She can't go on. The* VISITOR *takes a sip of
                champagne, smiles weakly and leaves.*)

                I blew it! I blew it!

                (DAN *pulls himself together.*)

DAN   No, no, no. You did very well under the
                circumstances. There'll be another day.
                (*Thinks.*) And another play . . . (*His tone tells
                us he may have seen the light about
                "Sewage".*)

GUNTER   The bride and groom approaching!

                (*Applause . . . chords of music . . . as* ZANA
                and RAFE *enter in full wedding splendour.*
                WEBBO *and* KOICHI *are in attendance.* ZANA
                has a bucket.)

ZANA   Right everybody. We've both peed in the
                bucket. See if you can separate the waters!

                (*She flings the contents at them . . . but it's a
                joke, as the bucket contains confetti.
                Everyone emerges from the cover they ran to.*)

                Fooled yer!

                (*Applause, jeers.* BILLY *is at the mike.*)

BILLY   We're gonna sing to you as promised. No
                apologies fer it bein' a piece o' Shakespeare.
                Nor fer it bein' a love poem. Let love preside
                this happy day.

BONNY   Sure will . . . sure will!

(*Now the music strikes up, which could be from musicians on stage as wedding guests.* BILLY *and the rest of the cast give a stirring, never mocking, rendering of Sonnet No. 18 in Country and Western style.*)

"Shall I compare thee to a summer's day?
Thou art more lovely and more temperate;
Rough winds do shake the darling buds of May,
And summer's lease hath all too short a date.
Sometimes too hot the eye of heaven shines
And often is his gold complexion dimm'd
And every fair from fair sometime declines,
By chance, or nature's changing course, untrimm'd;
But thy eternal summer shall not fade,
Nor lose possession of that fair thou ow'st;
Nor shall Death brag thou wanderest in his shade,
When in eternal lines to time thou grow'st.

(*The tempo slows for a big finale.*)

So long as men can breathe, or eyes can see,
So long lives this, and this gives life to thee.

(KOICHI *and* WEBBO *now come to the mike.*)

KOICHI

Now we poor spirits with powers waning
Must mortal be. No use complaining.
Where we once made and un-made confusions,
You make them now and you have no illusions.

WEBBO

And where you once sought blessings from
             the elves
Now you, and you alone, must bless
             yourselves.
So wish tonight, in every theatre, every hall,
Peace, life, love, laughter . . . happiness to all!

(*All sing a reprise of the last two lines of the song as the lights fade to black.*)

MUSIC

I'm indebted to Tim, Larry, Megan and Don for helping me get the music together.

GUNTER'S German song in Act Two is not included but is available on cassette: "Berlin by Night". (EMI No. TC - EMS 1395.)

When BONNIE and DAN enter singing an old Tennessee love song, I suggest "The Tennessee Waltz".

Note that for "Nonny Nonny No", we do not provide music for the verses, which are spoken rhythmically to a jazz beat intro on drum, base or whatever you have. The tempo can vary to aid expressing the words in a mocking style. BONNY takes the verses except for the lines marked for ZANA and MIRA. All take the chorus.

DINNER AT THE DUCK

If you're lookin' for a place to eat I'm tell-in you that you're in luck—

Eve-ry-one on the Stratford beat has din-ner at the Duck

Oh — people all a-round the world know this hos-tel-rie from

Sid-ney, Stut-gart, Paris, Rome Tok-y-o and New York City 'cos Here's the place

you'll see the stars having din-ner at the Duck— Come and mingle

in the bars din-ner at the Duck— where eve-ry night is an

op-en-ing night and your taste buds get stage struck! Well! Quack quack quack quack quack

& din-ner at the Duck— Din-ner din-ner din-ner at the Duck

Din-ner you won't get thin-ner Din-ner at the Duck!

Ham-let, Fal-staff Ros-a-lind They're all ea-ten here

You may see Cor-de-li-a 'ou-yin' a beer for ol King Lear!

Sit right down and take your ease for din-ner at the Duck—

CHORUS – NONNY NONNY NO

Hey non-ney non-ney   The sin-gle life is bon-ny!   So
if he asks you ho-ney say— non-ney non-ney no! no-ney no

non-ney no   (yeah) If he asks yer
ho-ney say   non-ney non-ney no!

you spotted snakes

billy: you spot-ted snakes   with dou-ble tongue
Dan:you spot-ted snakes   with dou-ble tongue, thor-ny
Hedge   frogs be not seen   newts and blind   worms do no
wrong   come not near our fai-ry queen   come
near   our fai-ry queen   come not near   our fai-ry
queen   newts and blind   worms do no wrong   come not
near our fai-ry queen